Women's Economic Empowerment

Inna Michaeli

Women's Economic Empowerment

Feminism, Neoliberalism, and the State

palgrave
macmillan

Inna Michaeli
Humboldt University of Berlin
Berlin, Germany

This book is based on the author's doctoral dissertation at the Humboldt University of Berlin, Faculty of Humanities and Social Sciences.

ISBN 978-3-030-89280-7 ISBN 978-3-030-89281-4 (eBook)
https://doi.org/10.1007/978-3-030-89281-4

This Palgrave Macmillan imprint is published by the registered company Springer Nature Switzerland AG.
The registered company address is: Gewerbestrasse 11, 6330 Cham, Switzerland

Preface

Many years ago, I received a voucher for a bookstore and bought a book called *Nice Girls Don't Get Rich: 75 Avoidable Mistakes Women Make with Money*. I was slightly embarrassed, as I expected superficial capitalist tips. In reality, I could really use some of those tips. There was a sense of comfort in the idea that my careless financial conduct had something to do with gender, and even more comfort in the promise that the situation might be fixable. This promise has never materialised for me. Perhaps nice girls really don't get rich after all.

Yet, the book got me thinking about economy and gender, and the frequent representation of women as inherently flawed economic subjects. Self-help best-sellers invite women to "lean in", with the promise that by changing ourselves, we can change our economic realities. How to reconcile this neoliberal trend with the long history of feminist scholarship and politics deeply critical of capitalism and patriarchy at the foundations of our societies? Making sense of this gap, I suspected, could teach us about the contemporary relationship between economy and gender. In other words, I became interested in the encounter between feminism as a theory and politics of social and economic justice, and the real, material survival of women in today's profit-driven and market-oriented societies.

The field of women's economic empowerment offered the ultimate empirical terrain for the investigation of this encounter and its contradictions. Women's economic empowerment, particularly via entrepreneurship training and microfinance, is promoted as a principal solution to gendered socio-economic inequalities, and debt is marketed as financial inclusion. Can empowerment truly offer substantial upwards mobility, or is it a neoliberal way for women to manage their own poverty? Engaging with material realities of women, primarily low-income, racialised and migrant women, grassroots economic empowerment projects surface the complexities of striving for socio-economic change in neoliberal times. It is a diverse field, encompassing feminist grassroots groups, international development agencies, state, inter-governmental and market institutions, with their different—at times opposing—ideologies and agendas. As a case study, the global project of women's economic empowerment invites a critical interrogation of the social, economic and political power structures within which the entanglements of feminism and neoliberalism take place, and individuals and institutions navigate their ways.

While multinational corporations champion women's empowerment, gender equality, and "girl power", millions of people are drawn into the terrifying depths of indebtedness and into precarious labour markets that are as gendered, as they are racialised and class-based. Global capital in the form of Northern-based corporations and private foundations increasingly takes a comfortable seat at the multi-stakeholder tables in institutions like the United Nations and the World Health Organization. This process is often driven by the assertion of compatibility of the interests of the people and the interests of global capital. Gender equality is portrayed as achievable in global capitalism, with just a bit more empowerment. With this book, I desire to surface the multiple conflicts and contradictions obscured in contemporary neoliberal arrangements, so that feminist analysis and emancipatory actions can better navigate the neoliberal debris of co-optation, complicity and resistance.

Berlin, Germany Inna Michaeli

Acknowledgements

My first thanks is to all the interview partners and practitioners who contributed their valuable time and knowledge to this research. I am most grateful to Prof. Dr. Gökce Yurdakul for the motivating and supportive supervision, intellectual and academic guidance, kindness and friendship, and for holiday dinners that felt like home in a new country. My deep appreciation and thanks also go to Prof. Adriana Kemp for her always-insightful comments, the sharpest analysis, and generous guidance. For the loving support throughout the years of this research, thank you to Shirly Shimony-Schubert, Sharon Mantel, Maayan Geva, Shira Havkin, Tamir Lederberg, Tanja Gangarova, and Raz Weiner. Pushkin the cat always enjoyed sleeping on my drafts. The Rosa Luxemburg Foundation granted a 3-year scholarship and provided a stimulating intellectual and political environment. The Humboldt University of Berlin provided a travel grant for the first fieldwork and a completion grant. I am grateful to my colleagues at AWID for a feminist and supportive workplace and for the privilege to support feminist efforts for macroeconomic transformation and learn from the brilliant feminists in this field. Finally, my great gratitude is to my dearest Pavlovs family: my brother Vladislav and my parents, Larisa and Michail, for teaching me what really matters. I stressed you big time when I dropped out of high school, but here we are.

Contents

About the Author

Inna Michaeli A feminist sociologist, Michaeli has researched and taught on identity and belonging, economic globalisation, theories of knowledge production and qualitative research methods. In 2017, she defended her doctoral dissertation on women's economic empowerment, on which this book is based, at the Humboldt University of Berlin. Inna Michaeli has been deeply involved in feminist, queer and social movements for over two decades. She works at the Association for Women's Rights in Development (AWID), a global feminist organisation.

Abbreviations

AEEW	Association for the Economic Empowerment for Women
AWID	Association for Women's Rights in Development
EC	European Commission
ESF	European Social Fund
EU	European Union
ICRW	International Centre for Research on Women
IMF	International Monetary Fund
ISI	ISI e.V. Initiative Selbständiger Immigrantinnen (association, Germany)
KIEDF	Koret Israel Economic Development Funds
LFA	Logical Framework Approach
M&E	Monitoring and Evaluation
MAOF	Business development centers in Israel, previously MATI
NGO	Non-governmental organisation
OECD	Organisation for Economic Co-operation and Development
SAWA	A direct non-bank loan fund by KIEDF (Israel)
SBA	Small and Medium Business Authority
SEWA	Self-Employed Women's Association (India)
SME	Small and Medium-sized Enterprises
USAID	United States Agency for International Development

CHAPTER 1

Introduction: Economic Empowerment Between Feminism and Neoliberalism

Women's economic empowerment is simultaneously a buzzword and a fascinating field at the intersection of some of the most pressing questions of our times: local and global economic inequalities, intersection of gender, race and class, the relation of civil society to the state and the market, to name a few. This field has undergone radical transformations over the past five decades. With its origins in feminist grassroots initiatives in Southeast Asia and Latin America, it became a global project, embraced by international financial institutions, governments and civil society. "Investment in women" is now celebrated as "smart economics". It is difficult to find a development agency, financial institution or a national economic authority without a reference to women's economic empowerment in their plans.

In contemporary public discourse, women's economic empowerment has become synonymous with microcredit loans for women in poverty, a seat in the corporate boardrooms for the wealthier women, and self-help bestsellers like Sheryl Sandberg's book "Lean In: Women, Work, and the Will to Lead", encouraging women to change our act in order to succeed in the workplace and the global market. These are all forms of individual intervention, whose effectiveness, as with microfinance, and whose relevance, as with leaning in, are extensively questioned by feminist scholars and practitioners. Yet, the origins of women's economic empowerment lie in feminist analysis and transformation of the structural, rather than individual, causes of economic inequalities.

I. Michaeli, *Women's Economic Empowerment*,
https://doi.org/10.1007/978-3-030-89281-4_1

In the earlier empowerment initiatives of 1970s through the 1990s, in the global South, feminists accounted for exploitative patriarchal and neo-colonial structures of society and economy, and approached economic empowerment interventions as part of broader agendas for social, economic and political transformation. With the globalisation of women's economic empowerment in the course of the 1990s and 2000s, and the entrance of powerful actors and institutions, the ideologies and practices inhabiting this field have multiplied and shifted greatly.

Globally, the vast interest and resources invested in women's economic empowerment appear to be a remarkable achievement of women's rights advocates. Initially local small-scale grassroots initiatives, women's economic empowerment programmes—particularly microfinance and micro-entrepreneurship schemes—enjoy worldwide popularity as a leading solution for social and economic advancement of women, especially of low-income, migrant and ethnic minority communities. International institutions such as the World Bank and the United Nations insistently promote women's economic empowerment programmes, and governments and civil society alike embrace them. In previous decades, development practitioners and scholars in areas like Women in Development (later evolving into Women and Development, Gender and Development) extensively problematised and protested the exclusion of women from international development programmes. Shouldn't the popularity of women's economic empowerment be celebrated as a feminist success?

In fact, this incorporation of women into globalised market economies has raised a whole range of critical concerns at the intersection of feminism and neoliberalism. If the exclusion of women from development agendas used to be the problem, today, the concern is not simply *whether* women are included, but *how* they are included. Which economic systems and paradigms do these agendas reaffirm? Who profits the most from microfinance programmes and who loses? Which gender norms and subjectivities do these processes of inclusion produce and reproduce? Consider, for example, the financialisation of women's economic empowerment. In her experiential account of empowerment, Srilata Batliwala (2007) noted the decline in sociopolitical aspects of empowerment in favour of large-scale microfinance programmes and so-called financial inclusion. While financial inclusion may intuitively sound like a good thing, in practice it means incorporation of people—overwhelmingly women and Black, indigenous and other racialised communities—as creditors in debt-based economies (Federici, 2014). Critical scholars of microfinance shift to speak of debt entrapment rather than credit. Until this day, there is no consensus or convincing evidence that the multi-billion endeavour of microfinance, with all its massive publicity, actually benefits the poor; but the evidence for its facilitation of indebtedness and expansion of globalised markets and consumerism is overwhelming (Karim, 2011; Hickel, 2017). Ultimately, these concerns question the accelerated inclusion and incorporation of social groups into the same economic and financial systems that dispossess, exploit and exclude them in the first place.

Ironically, the successful globalisation of women's economic empowerment was enabled and driven by its commercialisation and commodification (Berkovitch & Kemp, 2010). Like other social economy initiatives, women's economic empowerment has been promoted and celebrated in free market terms and values, such as profitability and return on investment, but was also increasingly subjected to this market logic and became dependent on it. Discourses of investment in women as 'smart economics' and the' business case' for women's rights—the idea that gender equality is economically profitable—won a new space for gender inequality in national and international policy debates and agendas. Yet, these discourses have also brought with them a reduction of women's economic rights to quantifiable economic returns and profitability conditioning, away from inalienable and unconditional human rights frameworks (Awori, 2017). Civil society actors, including the women's rights organisations who have embraced these discourses, became more or less willing participants in the process of neoliberal expansion of market values and logics into social economy and social change spheres. Of course, the other side of this expansion has been the systematic elimination of alternative, non-capitalist forms of social and economic thought and action.

How are we to understand this subordination of initially feminist projects to market logic? Notably, the feminist theorist Nancy Fraser (2013, 2017) has argued that feminism engaged in what she calls a dangerous liaison with neoliberalism, in a way that ultimately contributed to its legitimacy. Central to this development, according to Fraser, is the feminist shift away from socialist critique of capitalism and its focus on "bread and butter" issues, to preoccupation with matters of culture, gender and identity. In Fraser's own terms, a shift from politics of redistribution to politics of recognition. This narrative of feminist history was strongly disputed on both empirical and theoretical grounds, from overlooking the multiplicity of feminist histories to dividing economic, cultural and political dimensions, contrasting a feminist critique of cross-cutting structures of domination (Butler, 2008; Aslan & Gambetti, 2011; Duggan, 2012). Fraser's narrative, perhaps the most associated with Western socialist feminism, was also criticised for lacking attention to feminist movements in the global South and scholarship by Black and post-colonial feminists, particularly at intersections of gender, race, colonisation and global inequalities (Bhandar & da Silva, 2013). Once we turn attention to this multiplicity of feminist geographies, politics and agendas, accusing the feminist movement for serving capitalism becomes even more problematic. As Aslan and Gambetti argue, following Chandra Mohanty, this is not only reductionist, but performs reduction in a very specific way: it reconstructs the feminist imagined community around a particular set of dominant feminist discourses in the global North, marginalising and rendering invisible all others. While we are undoubtedly witnessing a strand of corporate or neoliberal feminism as a distinct form of contemporary feminism (Rottenberg, 2014), simplistic narratives about a presumed overtake of feminist movements and feminism itself are clearly not satisfactory. In recent years, the feminist conversation on feminism and neoliberalism has sought to move beyond the simplistic co-optation and resistance dichotomy (Eschle & Maiguashca, 2018), a conversation to which this book aims to contribute.

The global project of women's economic empowerment, I suggest, has an insightful story to tell and a contribution to make. Critical scholars researching women's economic empowerment and microfinance in concrete historical and political contexts have offered a far more nuanced analysis of entanglements between feminism, neoliberalism and the state (Maclean, 2013; Sa'ar, 2016; Kemp & Berkovitch, 2019), and the gendered and racialised dynamics in operation (Hossein, 2016). In this research, I chose to focus on grassroots non-governmental organisations (NGOs) founded by and for women from diverse racialised, ethnic, national and socio-economic identities, trusting to find in such feminist initiatives a level of agency, self-critique and reflexivity. One can reasonably assume that a level of complicity with neoliberalism might be unavoidable in projects that are ultimately about integrating women as entrepreneurial subjects in market economies. Yet, rather than projecting ready-made critiques of neoliberalism on these NGOs, my aim was to learn from them and from their everyday practice of navigating the complexities and contradictions inherent to economic empowerment. As Caroline Shenaz Hossein notes, often "microfinance's advocates and its critics tell a generic story of commercialization, while failing to examine intersectional identities and the people who run these programmes" (Hossein, 2016).

Similarly, Adriana Kemp and Nitza Berkovitch point out that the mezzo level of analysis—management and staff of the NGOs—enables us to capture "how they actually 'do' both feminism and neoliberalism, continuously entangling and disentangling the two" (2019: 14). I examined, in other words, how these organisations encounter and cope with the tensions of feminism and neoliberalism in the practice of economic empowerment, in training women to become entrepreneurs, and in accompanying them to access microfinance services. How are institutional relations among civil society, state, and market formed in this field? How can we understand the global project of women's economic empowerment against the backdrop of profoundly unequal, racialised and gendered national economies? Inspired by institutional ethnography as a methodological framework committed to producing sociological knowledge "for the people" (Smith, 2005), my purpose was to interpret, contextualise and theorise the problems and challenges in the field, in order to produce knowledge of value and relevance not only for scholars but also for the practitioners.

Empowerment in itself appears to be an unquestionably noble cause, commonly understood as an essentially good process. However, critical scholars have pointed out that rather than being good or bad, empowerment is inherently a relationship of power (Cruikshank, 1999). Through its intensive training programmes and disciplinary practices, empowerment programmes alter (or, rather, seek to alter) women's consciousness and sense of self, their ways of thinking, their social and economic behaviour, and their relation to the world around them. Empowerment aims to enhance women's capacity to act upon their self-interests, but it also partakes in constructing and defining these interests. In this perspective, empowerment can be analysed as a neoliberal technology of citizenship that works to produce certain kinds of citizen-subjects. Women's economic empowerment can thus be understood as one particular field, among many, where citizens and citizenship is constituted. The language of citizenship, as we shall see, becomes particularly critical when national contexts of economic empowerment are examined.

While women's economic empowerment is a broad field, encompassing activities like vocational training and economic literacy, two of its elements—microfinance and entrepreneurship training—make for particularly popular and interesting strategies. As noted, microfinance has been heatedly debated and interrogated for its questionable impact on people's lives on individual and systemic scale, such as its abovementioned functionality in incorporating marginalised communities into debt-based economies. Yet, its continued unprecedented popularity as the preferred financial model for women's economic empowerment, and its reincarnation and rebranding in terms like financial inclusion of women in market economies, call for a critical examination. Despite, or perhaps because of, its global popularity as a form of women's economic empowerment, the microfinance model is rooted entirely in neoclassical economics, and is uninformed by feminist economics. Why women's economic empowerment is so detached from feminist economics is a question I interrogate further.

Gender in microfinance is a good example of empowerment's productive power in constituting particular subjectivities and norms of social and economic life. One promise that the contemporary field of women's economic empowerment holds is that by changing themselves, women can change their economic realities. In other words, women appear to be doing something wrong, something that prevents them from becoming a proper economic subject, a classic *homo economicus*. Yet, interestingly, women also constitute the vast majority of microcredit recipients. Microfinance (called microcredit or micro-lending) institutions have always perceived women to be more reliable and trustworthy when it comes to credit repayment and to the investment of their earnings for the benefit of the entire family and community. In 2017, of the 9 million creditors of the Grameen Bank, the world's most famous and perhaps most infamous microfinance institution, 97% were women. Women emerge simultaneously as the flawed economic subject who needs fixing (be it via empowerment, business training or just a bit of leaning in) and as the proper gendered subject, expected to properly repay her loan and put her earnings into the family. In this line of thinking, women are a safer bet for debt, their family and community roles and ties make it more difficult for them to run away, default and disappear, and in some cultural contexts, to dishonour their family and community by failing to repay the credit. We can already note many problematic patriarchal, heteronormative and binary gender assumptions and norms regarding women, households, family and community emerging from such microfinance and empowerment frameworks.

Entrepreneurship training is interesting to us here not merely for its popularity, but for exceeding the scope of economic activity and constituting a form of subjectivity. The entrepreneurial, self-enterprising individual, reliant primarily on themselves rather than making claims on the state or community, is a neoliberal subject (Ong, 2006). When women, migrants and ethnic minorities are encouraged to become entrepreneurs as an alternative to the discrimination, exclusion and exploitation they encounter in local and transnational labour markets, the onus is on them to make ends meet, rather than on the state to restructure the labour market so that it offers adequate opportunities for all. To become an entrepreneur is not to simply acquire a set of tools and professional knowledge. It is to acquire, or engineer, a particular sense of self, with distinctive ways of thinking, experiencing and relating to the world. This includes self-management of one's own vulnerability, exclusion and oppression. As Boeri (2018) demonstrates, the framing of women informal workers as entrepreneurs can serve to obscure the exploitative features of this work: bearing the costs of production becomes investment, losing clear distinction between work and leisure time becomes autonomy. We can thus understand empowerment through entrepreneurship training as a project of constructing entrepreneurial, self-enterprising, and—ultimately—neoliberal subjects.

Considering that across national contexts, empowerment programmes' participants are primarily low-income, migrant, indigenous and otherwise racialised women, we can account for the gender, nationality, race, ethnicity, class and other dimensions in this neoliberal construction of citizens and citizenship. This is important because as Siddhant Issar (2021) notes in his work on racial capitalism, the most prominent accounts of neoliberalism and neoliberal subjectivity, such as those offered by David Harvey and Wendy Brown, speak from a universal subject position, insufficiently accounting for the gendered, racialised and class-specific constructions of neoliberal subjectivity, as well as one's lived experience in neoliberalism.

Initially implemented in the global South, women's economic empowerment initiatives mushroomed in the global North, so that paradigms, concepts and practices are imported, but also changed and adjusted in the course of this globalisation. Women are still targeted as the main audience, for grassroots initiatives of economic empowerment as well as for top-down institutions—100% of Grameen America debtors are women. In global South countries, these are often rural and low-income women. In global North countries, these are women from communities on the margins or outside the formal labour market, predominantly racialised and ethnic minorities and migrants. This may seem as an interesting course of globalisation, as market expansion generally moves from North to South. The complexity of course exceeds a one-way direction. Globalisation of a phenomenon can entail a heterogeneity of elements pursuing different if not contradictory aims. A microfinance institution expanding its operations from South to North may seek to expand its pool of potential debtors, effectively targeting "South in the North" when aiming to reach low-income, often Black, indigenous, ethnic minority or migrant women. A feminist collective that learns from empowerment practices of another feminist collective in a different country is likely to be driven by a different motivation, political rationale and objectives. Similarly, social movements in the North, such as anti-austerity movements, are inspired by and learn from the debt cancellation movements in the global South (Federici, 2014). Hence, speaking of globalisation of women's economic empowerment, we speak of globalisation of methods, interventions and emancipatory practices, on the one hand, and of globalisation of markets, complex institutional dynamics, and indeed politics of co-optation, on the other hand.

Since the 1990s, scholars have emphasised the need to examine local discourses and practices of empowerment as always embedded in regional, national and global relations of power (Parpart et al., 2002). The research on women's economic empowerment tends to be either too local or too global, examining either the particularities of local projects or global trends at a higher level of abstraction—a gap I strive to address. As the field of women's economic empowerment itself, this study is both global and local. To complement the discussion of women's economic empowerment as a global project, I take a closer empirical look into the German and Israeli fields of women's economic empowerment, as two comparable models of citizenship grounded in race and ethnicity as the base of the nation, and in their colonial past and present, respectively. This comparative perspective brings forth the relations among the economic, gendered, racialised and ethno-national dimensions of citizenship. In other words, it examines the globalised encounter between feminism and neoliberalism as always grounded in concrete political regimes of citizenship. Regimes that are gendered and racialised in their own particular ways, and that are embedded in the neo-colonial global economy, with its architecture of financial and inter-governmental institutions.

Policy-makers often speak of the economic participation of migrants and racialised and ethnic minorities, particularly women, as constitutive of a broader social inclusion and integration in society. For example, the European Social Fund (ESF)—the main instrument of the European Union to secure employment for its citizens—states in its rationale that "employment is the most effective way of giving people independence, financial security and a sense of belonging", explicitly linking employment and citizenship. The accompanying illustration video on the ESF website clarifies that ESF "works to get people skills, not benefits", leaving little doubt as for the negative value and implicit stigma prescribed to benefits and welfare. Meanwhile, the labour force participation of women from racialised communities and ethnic minorities is widely perceived as an indication of successful integration in the majority society—not only integration of individual women, but also of their families and communities. Critically, this promise does not entirely materialise. To illustrate, in Germany and France, women workers of Muslim faith who wear headscarves do not enjoy social inclusion on the grounds of their employment. On the contrary, in several regions they are legally excluded from certain forms of employment such as teaching, and by extension excluded from public life and national belonging (Korteweg & Yurdakul, 2014). It is not coincidental that in recent years in the European Union, a number of publicised court cases of discrimination against Muslim women who wear headscarves had to do with workplace discrimination and exclusion from the labour market. The labour market is a central field where forces of inclusion and exclusion play out.

When scholars and practitioners focus on dynamics of inclusion and exclusion, they run the risk of normalising and essentialising the economic and political structures themselves—be it the labour market or the nation-state. The focus on exclusion of particular social groups, while important, may problematise the exclusion itself, and assume the problem can be fixed with interventions of inclusion or empowerment of those excluded. Yet, inequalities never simply exist out there as a natural world order; they are created and perpetuated. Crucially, both discourses of (economic) empowerment and discourses of citizenship construct women and migrant, indigenous, racialised and otherwise marginalised communities in terms of lack and deficiency, as analysed by Barbara Cruikshank (1999) and Lana Tatour (2019), respectively. Such discourses imply that by addressing this deficiency, these groups finally get an equal chance at the labour market, or can reach a full egalitarian citizenship as its ideal promises. Rather than further upholding either empowerment or citizenship as normative concepts and desirable political projects, these critical scholars problematise them as systems of power and domination. Historical exploration is key. Rather than taking empowerment programmes for marginalised citizens as a starting point and asking whether one or the other empowerment method works, we must first ask why and how have certain social groups and communities become marginalised and disempowered to begin with? Which economic, political and sociocultural forces maintain the power structures that normalise dispossession, debt and poverty for some and unfettered accumulation of wealth for others? Indeed, one of the questions this book seeks to answer is how are we to understand the trend for empowerment in realities of perpetual and profound disempowerment.

The global project of women's economic empowerment has become synonymous with advancing women in the economy, but feminist efforts to transform the economy are far greater in scope and depth. While economic empowerment preoccupies itself with microeconomic shifts for individual participants, feminists have long investigated and scrutinised macroeconomic systems and the root causes of women's subordination in the economy. Aside from the thriving field of feminist economics, feminists are at the forefront of many social and economic justice movements. Feminists organise to transform economic systems and policies, from the undemocratic rule of international financial institutions like the International Monetary Fund and the World Bank to policy change campaigns on local and global levels. One recent example is the mobilisation for Convention 190 of the International Labour Organisation won in 2019, the first treaty to recognise the right of all to work free from violence and harassment, including gender-based violence, and including spheres of informal work. Another example is the feminist mobilisation for tax justice around transformation of tax systems and prioritisation of public services. Yet another is around corporate accountability and the mobilisation for a gender-responsive legally binding United Nations treaty on transnational corporations and human rights. Women are at the forefront of many mobilisations for climate justice, and call attention to the disproportionate impacts of the profit-driven climate crisis on the lives of women and peoples in the global South. All of this is to recall that despite the growing interest in the neoliberal entanglements with feminism—an interest to which this book responds—we must not let out of view the multiple and powerful ways in which feminists do resist economic injustices and corporate capture of gender equality (Gregoratti, 2016). Women's economic empowerment is not the strongest illustration nor the avant-garde of feminist action to transform the economy and make it work better for women; far from it. Rather, it is a powerful case study to learn about the constraints, dynamics and contexts of a feminist institutional action in neoliberal times. And, as a field that engages with low-income women, it does not have the privilege to escape the messy contradictions of everyday survival into abstract theory and neat political solutions.

In recent years, the economy features on feminist agendas with accelerated force and relevance. Even in the wealthier countries, the rollback on welfare, privatisation of social services, and the growing gaps between rich and poor have pushed women's rights organisations to re-engage with the economy. The heavily gendered, racialised and class-based inequalities of the dominant economic system are reaffirmed once again with the latest devastating economic effects of COVID-19 pandemic. Already in the early months of the pandemic, the International Labour Organisation (ILO) warned that out of the millions of jobs lost, women are the majority of the affected. Gender-specific forms of survival as well as exploitation in the constantly changing global economy are vividly captured by scholars and by social movements. Feminist movements develop new ways of activism and collective action, responding on the ground to these new cartographies and structures of economic oppression and injustice. New forms and strategies of feminist and political agency emerge. Theory and scholarship are trying to catch up with the practice, be it around the formation of transnational feminist networks (Moghadam, 2000) or the theorisation of the complex challenges that the practitioners of women's economic empowerment grapple with and try making sense of (Nagar & Raju, 2003).

Civil society can be a rather obscure term; for the purposes of this book, examination of civil society is in essence a study of individuals coming together outside formal political party politics and outside market institutions in an effort to influence social reality. Yet, as we shall see, this outside position is compromised from the outset, as civil society organisations—in our case, women's economic empowerment NGOs—re-engage with state and market institutions, create various hybrids, and redefine each other in the process. Civil society thus serves as an analytical term to capture institutional dynamics, yet it does not presume any unified, coherent and neatly delineated realm. Simply put, I am interested in the possibilities and limitations of institutional collective action to make a difference in neoliberal times, when economic alternatives are desperately sought for, yet are still so difficult to imagine. Can grassroots organisations concerned with making change in women's lives via economic empowerment correspond with what the feminist economic geographers J. K. Gibson-Graham (1997) called a politics of possibility, a creation of a different social reality, and if not—why? Learning from this case study, how can we better comprehend the role of civil society in establishing the hegemony of neoliberalism, a task identified as urgent by critical scholars (e.g., Plehwe et al., 2007)?

Notes on Theory and Methodology

Women's economic empowerment is a project that can be read—and has been read—through different disciplinary trajectories. Theories of civil society; studies in economic and political globalisation; feminist economics; sociological critique of neoliberalism, gender and citizenship; heated scholarly arguments over microfinance; research on entrepreneurship (and specifically female entrepreneurship and immigrant entrepreneurship); and, of course, all this scholarship in global as well as German and Israeli contexts is relevant to this research project. Following Smith's methods of institutional ethnography, I looked up to the initial empirical data for my decisions on best-suited theoretical frameworks. This guidance was provided by the problems, dilemmas, frustrations and dreams of practitioners and participants in the field, as I encountered them. Although it is a buzzword, or perhaps because of it, "women's economic empowerment" does not carry the same conceptual and practical meaning for all stakeholders involved in it (Sa'ar, 2014). Dissecting the term, we discover radically different meanings and diverging systems of knowledge production around each of the three components making this term: women/gender, economy and empowerment. Ultimately, three main overlapping corpuses of literature came together as the theoretical framework for this research. First, the entanglement of neoliberalism and feminism, not as a unified body of literature, but a set of theoretical strands developing around the interconnections of neoliberalism and feminism as analytical concepts. Second, empirical and theoretical research on women's economic empowerment. Third, the emerging field of critical entrepreneurship research, informed by post-structural theory while also rich in empirical data. Given the significant overlap among these corpuses, the analytical boundaries between them are rather provisional. Theoretical approaches like post-structuralism and concepts of hegemony, globalisation and gender cut across much of this literature, and help make sense of the empirical findings.

Knowledge is power, and in women's economic empowerment, multiple forms of knowledge and regimes of truth—about gender, economy, and socio-economic hierarchies of race, ethnicity and class—are enacted. The vast body of research produced by institutions such as the World Bank, for example, suffices for a number of lifetimes, and beyond its value as a source of empirical data, it constitutes a powerful scientific and policy discourse that influences realities across different regions of the world. The embrace of women's economic empowerment by development agencies and international financial institutions has generated extensive knowledge within distinctively neoliberal and neo-colonial epistemological foundations. Similarly, sociological knowledge about colonised and otherwise racialised social groups is not neutral, and is a tool of domination (Sabbagh-Khoury, 2021). Throughout this research, I strove to maintain awareness to the institutional interests invested in the production of knowledge about economic empowerment and to centre feminist, indigenous and otherwise subaltern sources and forms of knowledge.

I entered the research by the method of exploration and discovery. Institutional ethnography is not only a set of methods, but rather a research paradigm, an epistemological and methodological approach to the production of knowledge. Smith refers to institutional ethnography as a "sociology for the people". It is relevant to note that she began developing this method of inquiry at the encounter point between her early training as a sociologist and her experience in the US women's movement of the 1960s. Smith aspired to develop a sociology that would not nest above people's own standpoints, fixing them as objects, and the sociologist as an external objective expert. Instead, institutional ethnography is grounded in the everyday lives of individuals involved in institutional settings. It builds on people's own knowledge and expertise of their everyday worlds, systematically extends this knowledge beyond their everyday experiences, and locates it in broader relations of social, economic and political power. In other words, institutional ethnography expands the scope of what is, and can be, visible to the individuals about their social settings. This sociological knowledge about larger institutional forces shaping these settings is then intended to travel back to the individuals inhabiting institutions—a knowledge they can then integrate in their everyday lives. If they are activists, it is a knowledge that may serve their efforts to transform their social settings.

This is a qualitative study, extensive desk research on women's economic empowerment as a global project, coupled with an ethnography of German and Israeli fields of practice. In the first round of ethnographic work, I have set out to map the field in each national context, its key actors and their interrelations: mapping the strategies, activities and outputs of relevant NGOs, as well as their funding sources and other types of institutional relations with state and market institutions. This round included methods of participant observation in relevant events, informal conversations and semi-structured interviews in the principal NGOs, and regular monitoring and analysis of documents, reports, newsletters and other relevant materials throughout the research period. I also examined existing data on the subjective experiences of women participants in empowerment programmes, by assessing existing research and reviewing materials available in the organisations themselves, such as publications and internal evaluation reports. I did not include in my interviews a significant number of self-employed women, and instead referred to the existing ethnographies of minority women entrepreneurs, such as the works of Andrea Bührmann (2010) in Germany and Amalia Sa'ar (2014, 2016) in Israel. This decision enabled me to focus primarily on the institutional relations and structures of the field and its practitioners, without losing sight of the experiences of its participants.

For a deeper and nuanced insight, the second stage of the ethnography zoomed in on the practice of one Israeli and one German NGO. I have chosen the leading organisations in their respective country in targeting minority women for economic empowerment through entrepreneurship training: *Initiative of Self-employed Immigrants—ISI e.V.* in Berlin and the *Association of Economic Empowerment for Women* in Haifa. I have chosen two grassroots organisations rather than agencies established by the state or municipal authorities, in order to maximise the focus on the role and agency of civil society initiatives established by and for women. These NGOs have also been chosen due to their relatively long time of operation and due to their focus on women immigrants, national and ethnic/racialised minorities and marginalised communities. Their work with women of different ethno-national identities rather than a single ethnic or national group has enabled me to examine politics of identity in a broader comparative perspective. It has shifted the weight of the organisation more in direction of the global project of women's economic empowerment, rather than grounding it in the context of local civil society organisations affiliated with a particular racialised/ethnic group. I conducted semi-structured interviews about the concerns, problems and challenges that the women in this field—trainers, business consultants, and managerial staff—experience in their everyday practice. I have invited interview partners to share their own reflection on broader contexts in which they operate: their relations with other institutions such as state and funders, internal organisational culture, communities and constituencies.

In terms of analysis, there are macro, micro and mezzo levels to this discussion. The macro level focuses on the institutional relations among the actors of civil society, state and market, on local and global levels. The micro level is the individual empowerment process—the construction of citizens, their subjectivities and their identities: empowered and entrepreneurial, gendered, racialised, national and so on. And, the mezzo level is that of practitioners navigating these institutional realities. Throughout the book, these levels of analysis are discussed both separately and in relation to each other.

Two methodological comments are in order. Firstly, the critique of methodological nationalism warns us about discursively reproducing nation-states as natural and self-evident entities (Wimmer & Glick Schiller, 2002). In the Israeli case, methodological nationalism would also mean reproducing an ongoing project of colonisation as natural and self-evident, while in recent years, the settler-colonial framework gains prominence in the analysis of Palestine and the Israeli state project (Al-Hardan, 2014; Rouhana & Sabbagh-Khoury, 2015). In the spirit of institutional ethnography, I approach national contexts from the perspectives of the practitioners in the field and their perceptions of social reality, and expand it to institutional analysis informed by these critical frameworks. Secondly, the field of women's economic empowerment is largely gender binary and heteronormative, as I demonstrate and discuss in several chapters. Although my ethnography included interviews with activists from a trans initiative in Israel and a lesbian network in Germany, the analysis presented here is eventually limited to the cis-gender and heteronormative areas of the field more than I would have desired. As LGBTIQ rights, like gender equality, become a source of legitimacy for neoliberal macroeconomic policies, it is a vital direction for future research.

What Comes Next?

Chapter 2 introduces women's economic empowerment and its globalisation from the South to the North. First, it traces the historical and political development of women's economic empowerment in the global South, its adoption by international and state institutions, and the resulting transformations in the meanings and practices of empowerment. It continues to identify key questions that feminist scholarship on empowerment from the South poses for the more recent adaptations of empowerment in the North, and highlights some of the main differences in context. Finally, it considers the future of empowerment in the global North by pointing out dual dynamics by which women's economic empowerment, particularly in the form of entrepreneurship training and microfinance, is increasingly questioned and at the same time increasingly institutionalised. It becomes evident that even as empowerment projects seem to decline, their characteristics appear to thrive and outlive them: self-empowerment, entrepreneurial subjectivity and action persist and rise to become prominent models of social life and economic activity in today's neoliberal societies.

Chapter 3 offers a macro perspective and examines the power relations among civil society, state and market institutions as they evolve in the field of women's economic empowerment. Methodologically, I approach citizenship as a dynamic re-organisation of institutional relations among civil society, state and market; a definition I adopt from the sociologist Margaret Somers. While women's rights organisations turned to entrepreneurship training as an alternative to making claims on the increasingly neoliberal state, they ended up re-engaging with the state and the market in a new kind of contract, and found themselves locked in a new constellation of power relations. In this neoliberal contract, new hybrids among civil society, state and market emerge, accompanied by a re-organisation of their roles. Crucially, institutional, bureaucratic and administrative mechanisms—such as Monitoring and Evaluation frameworks—regulate the relations among institutions. These technical mechanisms may seem entirely non-political; yet, they effectively mitigate potential political and ideological tensions among the actors, and ultimately act to de-politicise their encounter and to prevent potential conflicts, ultimately establishing a permanent state of consensus, taken here as a neoliberal form of power. Indeed, what makes this contract distinctively neoliberal is not just its content, but also the way by which neoliberal hegemony is achieved: through an increasing shift from coercion to consent-based institutional dynamics. We can see how civil society organisations play an active role in the establishment of the neoliberal hegemonic order, while repeatedly running across technical—yet, essentially, political—obstacles in their attempt to address social and economic inequalities.

Chapter 4 reveals that even for the feminist organisations in the field of economic empowerment, the premises of neoclassical economics and financial capitalism remain largely unquestioned, in discourse and in practice. Why is the discipline of feminist economics, a feminist way of understanding economic and social life, almost entirely absent from women's economic empowerment? The rule of neoclassical economics reinforces an ontological divide between economy and society—the latter is interrogated critically for its gendered inequalities while the former enjoys its unshakeable domination as value-neutral, scientific and objective.

Taking the exceptionally high interest rates of microcredit (often much higher than the average bank loan!), I unravel the logic and political assumptions behind some of the financial taken for-granted of the field. Not all practitioners share this logic, but those who don't, struggle to find ways to contest the economic common sense of the field and to articulate counter-logics. Finally, the chapter reflects on the absence of feminist economics not only from the practice of women's economic empowerment, but also from the many critical accounts of entrepreneurship that deconstruct gender, yet allow the economic and financial aspects to go unquestioned.

Chapter 5 invites to shift from a macro perspective on institutional relations to a micro perspective on the construction of the citizens themselves, in their gendered and racialised/ethnic configurations. Considering the classic representations of entrepreneurs as predominantly white and male, I examine the emerging representations and role models of the female and the immigrant entrepreneur, and discuss where migrant, indigenous and ethnic minority women—the main clients of the empowerment programmes in question—are in this story. The reality of necessity-driven entrepreneurship in the grim absence of decent employment opportunities for marginalised women is examined against the expectation for individualistic "personal spark", entrepreneurial spirit and motivation the entrepreneur is expected to display. Then, empowerment and entrepreneurship-training curriculums are examined as technologies of citizenship applied to migrant and ethnic minority women. Through this detailed look at the curriculums, we come to comprehend the concrete processes and methods by which the construction of citizens operates, centring women's own agency vis-à-vis the aspirations of empowerment programmes. The method of consciousness-raising, central to the Western second-wave feminism, takes a different form in these curriculums. What is revealed is an institutional pressure to contain the effects of empowerment, in order to achieve concrete outcomes like income generation, but not, for instance, organising for political change. In a way, this is a reflection on the changing nature of relations among the personal and the political in neoliberal constrains of feminism. While the personal has always been political in feminist thought and practice, the neoliberal approach reduces the political to the personal.

Chapter 6 grounds the global, macro and micro levels of analysis of women's economic empowerment in concrete political contexts of citizenship. Considering the structural discrimination against racialised, ethnic and national groups in societies as also reflected in their labour markets, this chapter juxtaposes programmes of empowerment with realities of disempowerment perpetuated by ethno-national citizenship regimes predicated upon privileging one ethnic group over others. I focus on German and Israeli contexts and examine empirical findings on women's economic empowerment in the context of labour market exclusion and the broader political projects of citizenship and their racial and gender politics. Examining the different levels of disempowerment women encounter—family, community, and the state, I show a systematic refusal of state actors to take responsibility for exclusion exercised by state and market institutions, while persistently evoking orientalist discourses of tradition and religion to transfer the responsibility onto marginalised women and their communities. This chapter aims to shed light on how economic empowerment of women operates in concrete national contexts and citizenship regimes that structurally, continuously and intentionally disempower the racialised, ethnic and national groups to which these women belong. It offers a critical assessment of the neoliberal promise of labour market participation—through economic empowerment, microfinance and other initiatives—as a means of achieving a more egalitarian inclusive citizenship.

Finally, Chap. 7 ties the multiple levels of analysis into a multi-layered story about gender and economy, and offers an account of the relationship among feminism and neoliberalism. It shows that contrary to rather popular accounts of neoliberal co-optation, the field of women's empowerment tells a different story. First, it is not a naïve story of co-optation, but of radical transformative beginnings and painful disillusionment with the very possibility for civil society to counter the surge of neoliberal policies, from erosion of welfare systems to the increased precariousness of the labour markets, leading feminists to seek alternatives to policy change. Secondly, it is a story embedded in the changing structures of citizenship, as feminist and women's rights movements cannot be understood outside of the broader context of civil society and its re-engagement with state and market institutions, in new, complex and at times elusive neoliberal arrangements. Thirdly, it is a story of a reconfiguration of relations between the personal and the political, going beyond mere neoliberal individualism at the expense of the collective action. The focus on individual transformation is not in itself neoliberal—consciousness raising and personal transformation have been instrumental to radical feminist projects; rather, it is the way in which it contains and limits the political. This is one of the many paradoxes in the field: civil society organisations recognise that the inequalities are structural, yet the only solutions they can offer are individual. It is a story that ties identity and economy together, defying analytical oppositions between identity politics and economy. Finally and perhaps most importantly, it is not a neat and coherent story, because careful attention to lived realities, experiences and challenges of feminist organisations makes reduction, as tempting as it may be, much more difficult. Rather, the story of feminist and neoliberal entanglements invites accountability for the immense scope and depth of challenges facing our efforts for social and economic change in this moment in history.

References

Al-Hardan, A. (2014). Decolonizing Research on Palestinians: Towards Critical Epistemologies and Research Practices. *Qualitative Inquiry, 20*(1), 61–71.

Aslan, Ö., & Gambetti, Z. (2011). Provincializing Fraser's History: Feminism and Neoliberalism Revisited. *History of the Present, 1*(1), 130–147.

Awori, S. (2017, July 24). How the 'Business Case' for Gender Equality Sidelines Human Rights. *openDemocracy.* https://www.opendemocracy.net/en/5050/gender-equality-neoliberal-business-case/

Batliwala, S. (2007). Taking the Power Out of Empowerment – An Experiential Account. *Development in Practice, 17*(4–5), 557–565.

Berkovitch, N., & Kemp, A. (2010). Economic Empowerment of Women as a Global Project: Economic Rights in the Neo-Liberal Era. In *Confronting Global Gender Justice* (pp. 176–197). Routledge.

Bhandar, B., & da Silva, D. F. (2013). *White Feminist Fatigue Syndrome.* Critical Legal Thinking. http://criticallegalthinking.com/2013/10/21/white-feminist-fatigue-syndrome

Boeri, N. (2018). Challenging the Gendered Entrepreneurial Subject: Gender, Development, and the Informal Economy in India. *Gender & Society, 32*(2), 157–179.

Bührmann, (A. D.). (2010). Das unternehmerische Leitbild in der Gründungsberatung. In A. D. Bührmann, U. L. Fischer, & G. Jasper (Eds.), *Migrantinnen Fründen Unternehmen: Empirische Analysen und Innovative Beratungskonzepte* (pp. 45–66). Rainer Hampp Verlag.

Butler, J. (2008). Merely Cultural. In K. Olson (Ed.), *Adding Insult to Injury: Nancy Fraser Debates Her Critics* (pp. 42–56). Verso Books.

Cruikshank, B. (1999). *The Will to Empower: Democratic Citizens and Other Subjects.* Cornell University Press. Reprint Publication Date 2019.

Duggan, L. (2012). *The Twilight of Equality?: Neoliberalism, Cultural Politics, and the Attack on Democracy*. Beacon Press.

Eschle, C., & Maiguashca, B. (2018). Theorising Feminist Organising in and Against Neoliberalism: Beyond Co-Optation and Resistance? *European Journal of Politics and Gender, 1*(1–2), 223–239.

Federici, S. (2014). From Commoning to Debt: Financialization, Microcredit, and the Changing Architecture of Capital Accumulation. *South Atlantic Quarterly, 113*(2), 231–244.

Fraser, N. (2013). *Fortunes of Feminism: From State-Managed Capitalism to Neoliberal Crisis*. Verso Books.

Fraser, N. (2017). *Feminism, Capitalism and the Cunning of History*. Routledge.

Gibson-Graham, J. K. (1997). The End of Capitalism (As We Knew It): A Feminist Critique of Political Economy. *Capital & Class, 21*(2), 186–188.

Gregoratti, C. (2016). Cracks in the Corporatisation of Feminism. *Globalizations, 13*(6), 922–924.

Hickel, J. (2017). *The Divide: A Brief Guide to Global Inequality and Its Solutions*. Random House.

Hossein, C. S. (2016). *Politicized Microfinance: Money, Power, and Violence in the Black Americas*. University of Toronto Press.

Issar, S. (2021). Listening to Black Lives Matter: Racial Capitalism and the Critique of Neoliberalism. *Contemporary Political Theory, 20*(1), 48–71.

Karim, L. (2011). *Microfinance and Its Discontents: Women in Debt in Bangladesh*. University of Minnesota Press.

Kemp, A., & Berkovitch, N. (2019). Uneasy Passages Between Neoliberalism and Feminism: Social Inclusion and Financialization in Israel's Empowerment Microfinance. *Gender, Work and Organization, 27*(4), 507–526.

Korteweg, A. C., & Yurdakul, G. (2014). *The Headscarf Debates*. Stanford University Press.

Maclean, K. (2013). Gender, Risk and Micro-Financial Subjectivities. *Antipode, 45*(2), 455–473.

Moghadam, V. M. (2000). Transnational Feminist Networks: Collective Action in an Era of Globalization. *International Sociology, 15*(1), 57–85.

Nagar, R., & Raju, S. (2003). Women, NGOs and the Contradictions of Empowerment and Disempowerment: A Conversation. *Antipode, 35*(1), 1–13.

Ong, A. (2006). *Neoliberalism as Exception: Mutations in Citizenship and Sovereignty*. Duke University Press.

Parpart, J. L., Rai, S. M., & Staudt, K. A. (Eds.). (2002). *Rethinking Empowerment: Gender and Development in a Global/Local World*. Routledge.

Plehwe, D., Walpen, B. J., & Neunhöffer, G. (2007). *Neoliberal Hegemony: A Global Critique*. Routledge.

Rottenberg, C. (2014). The Rise of Neoliberal Feminism. *Cultural Studies, 28*(3), 418–437.

Rouhana, N. N., & Sabbagh-Khoury, A. (2015). Settler-Colonial Citizenship: Conceptualizing the Relationship Between Israel and Its Palestinian Citizens. *Settler Colonial Studies, 5*(3), 205–225.

Sa'ar, A. (2014). Economic Empowerment of Low-Income Women: A Mediating Concept in Competing Definitions of Reality. *Theory and Criticism, 42*, 151–174.

Sa'ar, A. (2016). *Economic Citizenship: Neoliberal Paradoxes of Empowerment*. Berghahn Books.

Sabbagh-Khoury, A. (2021). Tracing Settler Colonialism: A Genealogy of a Paradigm in the Sociology of Knowledge Production in Israel. *Politics and Society*. https://doi.org/10.1177/0032329221999906

Smith, D. E. (2005). *Institutional Ethnography: A Sociology for People*. Rowman Altamira.

Tatour, L. (2019). *Citizenship as Domination: Settler Colonialism and the Making of Palestinian Citizenship in Israel*. Available at SSRN 3533490.

Wimmer, A., & Glick Schiller, N. (2002). Methodological Nationalism and Beyond: Nation–State Building, Migration and the Social Sciences. *Global Networks, 2*(4), 301–334.

CHAPTER 2

The Globalisation of Women's Economic Empowerment

A practitioner in a women's economic empowerment organisation in Germany shared: "[S]ometimes people of senior age come to us, they have money, they want to support social projects, but they have this perception as if we are in Bangladesh. So that you give [women] one thousand euro and they will start a business. And we are in Germany, for a thousand euro there is no… we say, to start a business you need at least ten thousand."

To understand current configurations of women's economic empowerment, and to get a sense of why German senior citizens would find microfinance for migrant women an appealing social cause, let us begin this journey at the origins of their presumed fantasy—in South Asia. Setting the historical and global context, we begin with a brief overview of women's economic empowerment, take note of its transformations across time and space, and account for the role of microfinance in its globalisation. Women's economic empowerment and its particular form of microfinance (previously addressed as microcredit or micro-lending) came to countries like Germany and Israel from the global South, where empowerment and microfinance programmes developed not just as a financial model, but also as a range of different ideological endeavours—to transform unequal gender relations, to alleviate poverty. Scholars note that empowerment today is used in many different ways (Batliwala, 1994; Kabeer, 1999; Parpart et al., 2002; Mosedale, 2005). It is a buzzword, but also a densely contested discourse. Different actors charge it with different meanings, from radical to liberal and conservative, from politicians and corporations to

I. Michaeli, *Women's Economic Empowerment*,
https://doi.org/10.1007/978-3-030-89281-4_2

social economy and economic justice activists and microfinance professionals (Sa'ar, 2014). This term, and this field of practice, converges different and possibly contradictory perceptions of reality and the root causes of socio-economic problems, as well as of desired policies and practices.

Women's empowerment intensively developed in the 1970s and 1980s in Southeast Asia and Latin America, initially positioning itself as a counter-discourse and alternative to the mainstream top-down approaches of international development in the global South. In the past five decades, scholars and activists have extensively criticised international development paradigms (also referred to as global development or economic development) on multiple accounts. These accounts range from imposition of Eurocentric models on local and indigenous communities (Munck & O'Hearn, 1999), to exclusion of women and their own definitions of development (Pala, 1977; Visvanathan et al., 1997), to development as neo-colonialism and cultural imperialism (Escobar, 1995, Rahnema & Bawtree, 1997). Arturo Escobar and other scholars associated with post-development thinking have scrutinised development ideologies, policies and practices for fixing European and North American economic, social and political models as the ultimate truths of what constitutes the development of human societies. The imposition of these models played, and indeed continues to play a role in sustaining Western economic and political domination in the regions of Asia, Africa and Latin America, primarily benefiting global North countries, corporations, and non-governmental organisations. Today, most development funding and humanitarian aid does not reach organisations based in the global South, and ends up in global North-based international organisations, service providers, and consultancy firms. In 2015, World Disasters Report estimated that local NGOs receive less than 2% of humanitarian funding, albeit they are the first responders on the ground and are best positioned to deliver the appropriate response. Of the development aid marked for gender equality, still less than 1% ends up in the hands of feminist and women's rights organisations (Miller & Jones, 2019).

In early 1970s, women were largely absent from development projects, and have embarked on their own paths of improving their life and conditions. One of the best-known pioneers of women's empowerment is SEWA: Self-Employed Women's Association, established in 1972 in Ahmedabad, India. SEWA, operating to this day, has become a model and an inspiration for many other associations to come, making it a suitable reference point. These early empowerment initiatives have incorporated economic dimension as central to their perception of empowerment, comprehending women's economic independence in family and society as integral to changing women's lives. Over time, programmes of explicitly economic empowerment for women were developed. As we shall see, the emergence and popularity of economy-focused empowerment programmes do not signal the absence of an economic dimension in the earlier programmes, but rather a decline in a more holistic approach, which did not separate economy as much from politics, society and culture.

SEWA grew out of the Textile Labour Association, in response to an appeal by a group of migrant women workers and their contractor. Employed as cart-pullers in Ahmedabad's clothes market, they were living on the streets and had hoped that the Textile Labour Association would help them to find housing solutions. From its inception, SEWA had a strong ideological base, as their own introductory text reads, and drew its inspiration from Mahatma Gandhi's leadership of a textile workers' strike in 1917. In particular, they relate to Gandhi's belief that a union should address the worker's life in a holistic way, not only in the factory but also at home. This ideological strand entails a comprehensive approach to workers' organising and encompasses both public and private spheres, assuming active membership in industrial and national politics. SEWA's first struggle was to register as a trade union, despite not having a concrete employer to make claims on, thereby already challenging the administrative categories of the state. Historically, SEWA viewed itself as both an organisation and a movement under women's leadership. Its agenda encompassed questions of women's representation in decision-making and policy-making, as well as the possibilities and the obstacle presented by globalisation and liberalisation. Its focus on developing women's grassroots leadership further emphasises the political origins of the movement. Hence, the focus on self-employment became a departure point for a broader world view and comprehensive agenda concerning the lives of women, not limited to income generation. In essence, this is a model of a politically active citizenship. The set of questions to evaluate the work of the organisation forms a holistic understanding what change looks like in women's lives, encompassing employment and income as well as nutrition, health, child-care, housing, ownership of resources, collective organising and leadership, individual and collective self-reliance and literacy. This comprehensive understanding of women's economic empowerment bears transformative implications for law, society, education, health, culture and politics. Nonetheless, the lively interest in SEWA from international development agencies and politicians like Hilary Clinton, who visited SEWA in 1995, was sparked by its microfinance initiative—the SEWA Bank, which seemed to fit well with the neoliberal agenda (Boris, 2017).

In the 1970s and 1980s, women's rights organisations in Asia, Africa and Latin America shared a common sense of empowerment as a form of profound and structural change, as a commitment to transform power on both personal and collective levels. Srilatha Batliwala notes that differences notwithstanding, this common sense was shared across national and regional contexts. "[A]ll efforts to conceptualise the term more clearly stressed that empowerment was a socio-political process, that the critical operating concept within empowerment was power, and that empowerment was about shifts in political, social, and economic power between and across both individuals and social groups" (2007: 559). In these revolutionary times of radical theories and powerful movements of women's rights, civil rights and social justice, Black power, post-colonial politics and LGBT liberation struggles, the concept of women's empowerment came to signify incorporation of feminist analysis into these transformative strands of thought and action.

By the 1990s, women's empowerment was no longer only a counter-discourse, or a local alternative to international development. Women's rights organisations, social movements and academic fields like Women in Development have long protested the exclusion of women from international development agendas. Eventually, they were successful in influencing the object of their critique. International development agencies have increasingly taken note of these critical themes, and have adopted and adapted the concept and practice of women's empowerment (Berkovitch & Kemp, 2010). Soon they were joined by banks, governments and international financial institutions as the World Bank and the International Monetary Fund (IMF). Women's economic empowerment has become a global project.

This globalisation of women's economic empowerment occurred within a broader shift in global economic and political systems. Neoliberal economic reforms of the 1970s and 1980s find a consolidated expression in the Washington Consensus, the economic reform agenda agreed in the late 1980s by Washington, D.C.-based institutions—the IMF, the World Bank and US Department of the Treasury. This agenda for conditional loans, intended for Latin American countries in economic crisis and for the global South at large, included deregulation of markets, privatisation of state enterprises, competitive exchange rates and other free-market ideas. Famously termed as market fundamentalism by the Nobel-winning economist Joseph Stiglitz, this agenda solicited extensive social critique and outrage at the brutal and exploitative nature of market economy, and its resulting increase in poverty and social distress. The Post-Washington Consensus rose in response to this critique, and compared to the earlier global promotion of unfettered free-market policies, has brought more attention to local socio-economic conditions and the disastrous social impacts of IMF's conditional loans and structural adjustments. The Post-Washington Consensus expanded role of the state in addressing poverty and social problems, eventually positioning the state as complementary to rather than competitive with free markets. Society became a more central object of economic research in financial institutions such as the World Bank, though this has not extended to critical interrogation of economy and finance by social sciences (Engel, 2008).

Labelled as neoliberalism with a human face, this consensus demonstrates the success of civil society, progressive and social movements on the Left in placing social problems on the international agenda, but also their limitations. Demands for equality and social justice have finally been acknowledged, but remained subjected to and dominated by the prevailing economic policies and practices, and the ideologies underlying them. To illustrate, in her case study of World Bank lending policy in Vietnam, Susan Engel has demonstrated a gap between the impact of Post-Washington Consensus on actual lending versus its impact on the discourse in the form of policy documents and research output. Ironically, the World Bank's embrace of progressive and society-oriented rhetoric could serve to legitimise the same old lending practices and to perpetuate the existing social and economic inequalities, rather than necessarily signalling any actual transformative change. More broadly, the Post-Washington Consensus enabled and signalled a shift from economic coercion to consensus-based strategies that draw legitimacy from society-oriented and social justice discourses (Engel, 2008). This is where gender equality discourse comes in.

The theme of women and gender equality has played, and continues playing, a central role in establishing the neoliberal economic order as sensitive and responsive to the social problems of our times. Elisabeth Prügl (2017) has shown how the growing body of gender research at the World Bank has contributed to the neoliberal consensus, in what she calls neoliberalism with a feminist face. The Bank has invested extensive efforts to establish empirical and discursive correlation between gender equality and economic growth, capitalism's foundational principle. The establishment of that correlation proved to be a challenge; yet, once established, it has informed the shifting relations among feminism and neoliberalism on a number of levels. Gender equality became an additional source and discourse of legitimacy for neoliberal policies. The field of gender equality has been altered by neoliberal logic and operation modes, as we have seen in the case of financialisation of women's economic empowerment. And, neoliberal feminism, or corporate feminism, which pursues gender equality within the constraints of the market, has risen to power and popularity globally (Rottenberg, 2014).

Contemporary definitions of women's economic empowerment often speak in terms of individual women's ability to compete and succeed in the market, as well as her capacity to make decisions. The earlier notions of transforming economic, social and political relations and systems of power are nowhere to be found. The International Centre for Research on Women, in its 2011 publication Understanding and Measuring Women's Economic Empowerment: Definition, Framework and Indicators, stated that "to succeed and advance economically, women need the skills and resources to compete in markets, as well as fair and equal access to economic institutions". ICRW is an example of an influential global actor in creating women's rights discourses at the intersection of international aid community, national politics, the academia, the civil society and the business sector. It is a global institute of research on women and poverty alleviation, based in Washington D.C. with offices in Kenya and India. Its Leadership Council counted (at the time of this research) a diversity of high-ranking members, including the economist and philosopher Amartya Sen, the Queen of Jordan, former and current presidents of major foundations, Finance Minister of Nigeria and a Special Adviser to the UN Secretary General. ICRW's Board of Directors counted members from multinational management consulting firm McKinsey & Company, a Senior Advisor to Hillary Clinton and an Executive Director of Oxfam International, in addition to senior journalists and academics. ICRW is a valuable example because it is not a conservative institution, but counts among its leaders several individuals and organisations explicitly committed to values of economic justice and gender equality. In ICRW's and similar definitions, the concept of power is not entirely absent, yet is understood as "the power to benefit from economic activities" rather than power to challenge, change and transform economic, social and political relations and systems of power. The main difference is that such contemporary definitions take the market economy for granted, as is also evident, for example, in the replication of the market language of competition. Empowerment is no longer about changing the economy, but about better surviving, navigating and competing in it.

The dominant discourses of gender equality and women's entrepreneurship similarly articulate longstanding feminist concerns within the constraints of neoliberalism, so that the market economy in itself is never questioned as the optimal, and indeed the only viable model of organising social and economic life. For example, a study conducted by the European Commission's Directorate General for Enterprise and Industry has identified several obstacles for women's entrepreneurship, particularly around women's access to finance (more about this topic in Chap. 4). The study speaks to "contextual obstacles" such as "educational choices, traditional views and stereotypes about women" and suggests that a change is desirable. Yet, all obstacles remain contextual, in no way structural or inherent to the market economy and financial institutions. Entrepreneurial and financial spheres are perceived and presented as gender-neutral, largely devoid of any gendered, racial and other relations and systems of power. While the European Union and its policy and research institutions have always articulated gender equality agendas in terms of market logic, scholars note recent escalation in market-oriented discourses and economic arguments for gender equality (Elomäki, 2015). Just as with the World Bank, the framing of gender equality discourse and agendas perfectly compatible with market economies serves to legitimise neoliberal economic models, policies and practices.

To summarise so far, the neoliberal turn in women's economic empowerment entailed a number of shifts: The focus of empowerment shifted from the collective to the individual woman. Economic well-being has become detached from broader feminist agendas that entailed transformation of sociopolitical relations and systems of power. The narrative of unquestioned compatibility of gender equality with market economy gained ground, largely owing to the insistent discourse generation and knowledge production by institutions like the World Bank and the European Union. All this is by no means unique to the field of women's economic empowerment. Processes of NGOisation throughout the global South but also globally, from professionalisation of social movements to the fragmentation of broad emancipatory agendas into constricted areas of work in order to fit narrow niches of philanthropy, are all characteristics of our times. In some parts of the world, civil society institutions have come to substitute declining state welfare mechanisms; in others, people never had a functioning welfare mechanism to rely on.

In this process of globalisation, the critical analysis of power was largely taken away from women's economic empowerment, its conceptualisation, practices, objectives and methods (Mosedale, 2005; Batliwala, 2007). As a result, little of the transformative potential of empowerment was left. Development agencies as well as financial institutions, governmental programmes and NGOs adopted the terminology but failed—if ever attempted—to address relations of social, economic and political power and to examine their own position in these relations. Women's empowerment was not only emptied out of its subversive content: it was actively charged with new—distinctively neoliberal and increasingly financialised—conceptualisations, practices, objectives and methods. These later economic empowerment and microfinance programmes in international development have largely focused on increasing one's income and thereby improving quality of life among its recipients and beneficiaries, without necessarily building their political capacity as citizens to challenge and change social, economic and political conditions. No more reliance on and claim-making towards the state; empowerment became about relying on oneself as an entrepreneurial and self-enterprising citizen, responsible for her own survival. Microfinance is one example. Another is the short-term entrepreneurship training courses aimed at engineering individual entrepreneurial behaviour, rather than long-term processes aimed at transforming consciousness and mobilising collective political action. Yet another example is setting objectives for monitoring and evaluation of empowerment programmes solely around income generation and loan repayments, rather than encompassing broader indications of positive change and setbacks in women's lives, rights and social status.

Criticisms of empowerment via microfinance emerged across geopolitical contexts against the backdrop of financialisation post-1990s, as the excessive focus on money came at the expense of gaining political control over resources and the power relations governing their distribution (Pereira, 2008). The focus on finance and income generation, detached from broader sociocultural and political aspects, has marginalised and silenced critical emancipatory themes of women's rights, from political agency to sexuality autonomy. Feminists have emphasised that money in itself, and the range of services and activities associated with microfinance, are acutely insufficient to transform women's lives, embedded in patriarchy and intersecting with other systems of power and inequality (Cornwall et al., 2008). Consider, for instance, income generation in patriarchal family structures where women do not have full control over the income they earn. While economic independence is surely an essential component of emancipation, if detached from a comprehensive analysis of women's lives, microfinance can reinforce patriarchal oppressive social order. Where microcredit schemes favour women as clients without careful attention to their sociocultural contexts, they have been noted to contribute to domestic violence (Hossein, 2016). Similarly, microcredit schemes that disregard the gendered division of labour can reinforce the traditional double burden: charging women with social expectations to perform both productive and reproductive labour. On the macro level, microfinance interventions fail to account for inequalities among social groups and countries and other structural factors that eventually generate economic marginalisation of the individual. In particular, the microfinance industry as such denies unequal distribution of wealth as the root cause for existing inequalities, or as a significant problem at all. The excessive focus on money is even more intriguing because, in colloquial terms, nobody is making big money here, at least not the women participating in microfinance and empowerment scheme. Microfinance institutions, banks, corporations and other actors are a different story. Indeed, I dropped very quickly one of my initial research questions—do economic empowerment programmes hold a potential for socio-economic mobility for the women participating in them? Even in cases of improvement in one's income, more often slight than substantial, there was never any promise of significantly transgressing boundaries of one's socio-economic class.

The de-politicisation of women's empowerment goes back to its globalisation and mainstreaming. Berkovitch and Kemp (2010) stress how the very conditions that facilitated the globalisation of women's economic empowerment via microfinance have eventually contributed to its commercialisation. Embraced by international financial and political institutions, women's economic empowerment became global and mainstream, but also commercialised. Like other social economy initiatives, women's economic empowerment has been promoted and celebrated in free-market terms and values, such as profitability and return on investment, but was also increasingly subjected to this market logic and became dependent on it. As microfinance and entrepreneurship-training as a form of empowerment for marginalised women increasingly became profit-making activities, even those practitioners and organisations that have previously operated according to different logics and ideologies, have themselves become subjected to market logic and market-based evaluation criteria.

Globalisation of women's economic empowerment entails globalisation of discourses and practices that do not only respond to women's economic needs: rather, they participate in the articulation of their needs and in the construction of their subjectivities. Critical research in recent decades has been profoundly influenced by the awareness that representational practices participate in the production of the subjects they claim to represent. With this awareness, critical scholars of empowerment and entrepreneurship have noted that as women entered development policies and practices, they encounter a range of gender norms informed by a set of assumptions about women, gender, family and society (Cornwall et al., 2008; Ahl & Marlow, 2012). This is a mixed set of sociocultural and stereotypes concerning gendered division of labour in the family and in society. What are some of the notions one encounters on a regular basis while reading publications and conversing with practitioners include? Women are better in repaying loans because they are more reliable, and are less inclined to run away and more prone to shame in case of failing to pay back. Women are better in repaying loans because they are more careful as entrepreneurs, not as risk-taking as men. Women develop carefully planned business plans and do not rush to look for big loans from the outset. Women are more inclined to invest in the family and the next generation and less likely to spend their earnings on themselves. While these notions sum up to making a case for investment in the empowerment of women, they also entrap women in binary and restrictive norms of gender and patriarchal division of labour and responsibility in the family and the community.

We have opened with the ironic point of a practitioner that the fantasy narrative of women's economic empowerment in Bangladesh does not really work in Germany. In reality, this narrative does not work too well in Bangladesh either. As Lamia Karim (2011) demonstrates in her thorough study of microfinance in Bangladesh, the massive machinery of knowledge production about microfinance filters out the extensive evidence on the limited benefits and the substantial harms of microfinance for individuals and communities. This machinery, operated and financed by INGOs, development agencies and international financial institutions, generates and sustains a false narrative of microfinance as a successful magic bullet against poverty, while in effect plunging impoverished women into spiralling debt, with multinational corporations as the main profiteers.

Despite this wealth of critique, a recent comparative multi-country research on women's empowerment in Latin America, the Middle East, South Asia, West Africa and the United Kingdom, conducted by a consortium of feminist researchers, indicates that many critical scholars and practitioners have not entirely given up on the transformative potential of empowerment in women's lives (Cornwall, 2014). Rather, researchers and activists repeatedly engage in constructive dialogue with different institutional actors, attempt to develop shared conceptual frameworks and to fulfil the promise of empowerment from a feminist perspective that maintains a critical stance towards neoliberalism and gendered and racial injustices. Critical scholars and practitioners take empowerment as a starting point to talk about its most downplayed dimension since the co-optation of empowerment by mainstream development: power.

As women's economic empowerment expands to the global North, Southern feminist critical engagement with empowerment, micro-entrepreneurship and microfinance offers urgent lessons and insights. The attention to local and global power structures that has accompanied empowerment discourses from their early times has recently re-surfaced in feminist debates with added rigour. Given its origins as an alternative to the neo-colonial top-down approaches of development, it is understandable that empowerment always maintained a strong connection to the local and insisted on attention to the agency of women in their immediate lived contexts and on their own terms. Yet, without dismissing the value of the local, scholars call attention to examining empowerment in the context of national and global relations and systems of power and the impact they are having on the lives of people presumed in need of empowerment (Parpart et al., 2002).

Attention to local and global relations and systems of power requires both a historical and a contemporary perspective. To become a beneficiary for empowerment one had to become disempowered in the first place. Not just as an individual, but as a member of a certain community, society, country and region. Which historical processes—over decades, centuries and generations—have produced the structural inequalities and the forms of injustice, discrimination, institutional and everyday racism and sexism people encounter in their economic and social life? Historical examination of power relations makes clear that disempowerment of social groups and communities is never a simply given condition; it is produced and reproduced and needs to be accounted for. Attention to power relations in the present also engages with a range of interconnected spheres and systems that individuals navigate in the course of their social and economic life. What happens, for example, when the state or the agency implementing or funding an empowerment programme for an indigenous or migrant population is also the perpetrator of injustice and discrimination against that same population? A state institution or the development agency may run or fund empowerment programmes without actually allowing them to acquire and exercise more power, economic or political (Mosedale, 2005). An authority or agency running or funding empowerment programmes, may genuinely be interested in women's increased self-reliance, to reduce welfare spending for instance, but may at the same time seek to constrain their collective action and political organising for their rights. In the context of specific citizenship regimes, where empowerment commonly targets migrant women and women from indigenous and migrant groups and racialised and ethnic minorities, some of the emerging questions are, is there a national interest, intention or even tolerance on behalf of the state for these social groups actually acquire more social, economic and political power? How do we understand a reality in which empowerment programmes supported by the state emerge simultaneously to persistent forces of discrimination, exclusion and marginalisation that are tolerated or even set in motion and perpetuated by the state? These questions are discussed in Chap. 6. Recognising the varied and outright contradictory meanings of empowerment, scholars offer ways to differentiate them. One such classification distinguished between liberal and liberating empowerment, "contrasting representations of empowerment as a gift that can be given with those that locate empowerment in deeply contested processes of structural change in power relations" (Cornwall et al., 2008: 3). What makes empowerment liberal, or neoliberal, is consensus on the changes that empowerment is expected to generate. It is not intended to bring about changes that might trigger major conflicts or power struggles. It is effectively contained, and is not transformative in a way that might get "out of control"—challenging the existing socio-economic and political order and hierarchies among social groups more than convenient or agreeable to the institutions involved. Chapter 5 examines these dynamics in action.

On the global scale, women's economic empowerment has been losing its fashionable momentum, amongst others in favour of large-scale microfinance programmes (Batliwala, 2007). More precisely, it might be losing its momentum as a specific type of intervention; yet as a discourse, it is shining bright as ever. Even microfinance, despite its popularity and appeal to powerful institutions, is increasingly under attack for failing to deliver, and its capacity to alleviate poverty is fundamentally questioned (Bateman, 2010). Yet, many civil society organisations continue viewing micro-entrepreneurship to be a valuable path for women to improve their economic situation, even if not suitable for all. Women's economic empowerment through microfinance and micro-entrepreneurship is in a dual and seemingly oppositional process. On the one hand, it is expanding to the global North and enjoys its favourable reception with a range of financial institutions. On the other hand, the disillusionment with microfinance as a magic bullet that can solve structural problems of poverty and injustice has been slow, but it cannot be ignored. To illustrate, in both Israeli and German contexts I documented a dual process of decline and institutionalisation. In Israel, the NGO *Sviva Tomechet* (Supportive Environment) established by women immigrants from the Former Soviet Union which ultimately supported low-income and minority women from diverse ethnic and national groups to become entrepreneurs, closed down in 2013, after ten years of operation. In Germany, *NIKE Polnische Unternehmerschaft e.V.* by and for Polish women entrepreneurs, closed down in 2014, after 13 years of operation. At the same time, processes of institutionalisation took place: a small microcredit programme in Germany was adopted and enlarged by the government and the EU (see elaboration in Chap. 3), and in Israel the entire structure of state support for small and medium businesses was re-organised, and a project of state cooperation with a microfinance fund for Palestinian women was launched.

Even as women's economic empowerment and microfinance appear to decline, their narratives, raison d'etre and practices appear to thrive, and might well outlive them. The concept of financial inclusion of women and marginalised communities is gaining momentum in the new gender equality discourses, firmly embedded in neoliberal economic policies and expansion of debt-based economies. The "business case" for women's rights, though forcefully questioned by feminists, continues dominating national and international policy conversations on gender equality. Self-help, empowerment and entrepreneurial subjectivity continue rising to become prominent models of existence, economic life and political logic in modern societies.

References

Ahl, H., & Marlow, S. (2012). Exploring the Dynamics of Gender, Feminism and Entrepreneurship: Advancing Debate to Escape a Dead End? *Organization, 19*(5), 543–562.

Bateman, M. (2010). *Why Doesn't Microfinance Work?: The Destructive Rise of Local Neoliberalism*. Zed Books Ltd..

Batliwala, S. (1994). The Meaning of Women's Empowerment: New Concepts from Action. In G. Sen, A. Germain, & L. C. Chen (Eds.), *Population Policies Reconsidered: Health, Empowerment, and Rights* (pp. 127–138). Harvard University, Harvard Center for Population and Development Studies.

Batliwala, S. (2007). Taking the Power Out of Empowerment—An Experiential Account. *Development in Practice, 17*(4–5), 557–565.

Berkovitch, N., & Kemp, A. (2010). Economic Empowerment of Women as a Global Project: Economic Rights in the Neo-Liberal Era. In *Confronting Global Gender Justice* (pp. 176–197). Routledge.

Boris, E. (2017). SEWA's Feminism. In B. Molony & J. Nelson (Eds.), *Women's Activism and "Second Wave" Feminism* (pp. 79–98). Bloomsbury Academic.

Cornwall, A. (2014). *Women's Empowerment: What Works and Why?* WIDER Working Paper 2014/104. WIDER: World Institute for Development Economics Research, United Nations University.

Cornwall, A., Gideon, J., & Wilson, K. (2008). Introduction: Reclaiming Feminism: Gender and Neoliberalism. *IDS Bulletin, 39*(6), 1–9.

Elomäki, A. (2015). The Economic Case for Gender Equality in the European Union: Selling Gender Equality to Decision-Makers and Neoliberalism to Women's Organizations. *European Journal of Women's Studies, 22*(3), 288–302.

Engel, S. (2008). The World Bank and Neoliberal Hegemony in Vietnam. In R. Howson & K. Smith (Eds.), *Hegemony: Studies in Consensus and Consent* (pp. 171–195). Routledge.

Escobar, A. (1995). Imagining a Post-Development Era. In J. Crush (Ed.), *Power of Development* (pp. 211–227). Routledge.

Hossein, C. S. (2016). *Politicized Microfinance: Money, Power, and Violence in the Black Americas*. University of Toronto Press.

Kabeer, N. (1999). Resources, Agency, Achievements: Reflections on the Measurement of Women's Empowerment. *Development and Change, 30*(3), 435–464.

Karim, L. (2011). *Microfinance and Its Discontents: Women in Debt in Bangladesh*. University of Minnesota Press.

Miller, K., & Jones, R. (2019). *Towards a Feminist Funding Ecosystem*. AWID.

Mosedale, S. (2005). Assessing Women's Empowerment: Towards a Conceptual Framework. *Journal of International Development, 17*(2), 243–257.

Munck, R., & O'Hearn, D. (1999). *Critical Development Theory: Contributions to a New Paradigm*. Zed Books.

Pala, A. O. (1977). Definitions of Women and Development: An African Perspective. *Signs: Journal of Women in Culture and Society, 3*(1), 9–13.

Parpart, J. L., Rai, S. M., & Staudt, K. A. (Eds.). (2002). *Rethinking Empowerment: Gender and Development in a Global/Local World*. Routledge.

Pereira, C. (2008). Appropriating 'Gender' and 'Empowerment': The Resignification of Feminist Ideas in Nigeria's Neoliberal Reform Programme. *IDS Bulletin, 39*(6), 42–50. Institute of Development Studies. http://bulletin.ids.ac.uk/idsbo/issue/view/52

Prügl, E. (2017). Neoliberalism with a Feminist Face: Crafting a New Hegemony at the World Bank. *Feminist Economics, 23*(1), 30–53.

Rahnema, M., & Bawtree, V. (1997). *The Post-Development Reader*. Zed Books.

Rottenberg, C. (2014). The Rise of Neoliberal Feminism. *Cultural Studies, 28*(3), 418–437.

Sa'ar, A. (2014). Economic Empowerment of Low-Income Women: A Mediating Concept in Competing Definitions of Reality. *Theory and Criticism, 42*, 151–174. (in Hebrew).

Visvanathan, N., Duggan, L., & Wiegersma, N. (1997). *The Women, Gender and Development Reader*. New Africa Books.

CHAPTER 3

The Neoliberal Contract: Civil Society, State and Market

Civil society in the global North initially turned to women's economic empowerment and micro-entrepreneurship as a grassroots alternative to making claims for social and economic rights and justice from the state; and yet, these civil society organisations have ultimately re-engaged with the state and the market in a close contract. This chapter focuses on the politics of this contractual re-engagement.

Women's economic empowerment as a field encompasses a range of institutional actors: civil society organisations specialising in economic empowerment, entrepreneurship training, and micro-credit provision; state and municipal authorities; public and private foundations; and, banks and other financing and for-profit institutions. Such heterogeneity implies intriguing encounters among institutions with seemingly contradicting ideologies and priorities, which the contract manages and regulates. The institutional actors in the field of women's micro-entrepreneurship can be categorised in the triad of civil society organisations, market institutions, and the nation-state, and, significantly, their various and at times unexpected hybrids. Microfinancing institutions for example can be non-profit or for-profit, resembling civil society or the market, depending on its national registration possibilities and restrictions, and other considerations. Building on the conceptualisation of this triad as the three main pillars of contemporary citizenship (Somers, 2008), I approach women's economic empowerment as a concrete field in which their interrelations play out in complex institutional politics, and, subsequently, as one of the

I. Michaeli, *Women's Economic Empowerment*,
https://doi.org/10.1007/978-3-030-89281-4_3

multiple sites where contemporary citizenship is constituted. Citizenship, in this context, is an analytical category that allows us to think through multidimensional institutional dynamics that create the economic and political conditions of membership, inclusion and exclusion in societies. It encompasses legal status and rights, as well as more elusive yet no less critical dimensions as belonging (Bloemraad et al., 2008).

When we categorise institutions into state, market and civil society, they do not fall into neatly divided unitary categories or carriers of fixed and clearly differentiated logics and ideologies. On the contrary, the penetration of market-centred ideologies and logics into all spheres of life is well noted by Somers and other contemporary scholars of neoliberalism (Duggan, 2012; Davies, 2016). We might assume that the banks would be concerned with making profit; the state with regulation and citizen welfare; and, civil society and non-governmental organisations (NGOs) with the common good. Such a priori assumptions would then limit ethnographic attentiveness to institutional practices that in effect deviate from these preconceived notions. Careful ethnographic analysis reveals that institutions do not necessarily function according to the fixed roles they are presumed to have, and that the agency of people operating within them is multi-fold and complex (Greenhouse, 2010). Institutions, as the people inhabiting them, are not free from internal contradictions. Indeed, studies of institutional interactions and interrelations in the era of neoliberalism show that institutional realities may entail a hybridity of logics and rationalities. Those instances of the unexpected and the surprising enrich a nuanced understanding of institutional processes and entanglements.

Why think of re-engagement of civil society with the state and the market in terms of a new contract? Social contract is a notion associated primarily with the Enlightenment Era and the works of Jean-Jacques Rousseau and other thinkers of the time. It invokes the early problem of legitimacy of state power and authority over individuals, which has preoccupied scholars of philosophy, society and politics for centuries. While not in direct dialogue with this early theory, I address transformations of power in contemporary market-centred societies, in its national and global configurations. The category of contract was brought to gender studies by Carol Pateman in her classic book *The Sexual Contract* (1988), with the recognition that contracts are as much about what's in them, as what is absent from them—the implicit order of things they reproduce. Pateman constructed a powerful argument on the dual role of patriarchy and gender relations in social contracts: the exclusion of women from allegedly universal social contracts, and their subordination through parallel and unspoken contractual orders. Pateman reveals that while social contracts are seemingly gender-neutral, they in fact involve gendered relations of domination and subordination, an insight I carry into my analysis of institutional interrelations. This is a particularly helpful insight for a field like women's economic empowerment, which is rich in unspoken assumptions on the gendered, as well as racialised and class-based, social and economic order of society. Lastly, the terminology of contract hints at the increasingly contractual nature of institutional engagements in late capitalism, and its theorisation, termed also as contractual or regulatory capitalism (Raco, 2013; Davies, 2016). Simply put, institutional relations in the field of women's economic empowerment, as in other fields, are extensively regulated by actual legally binding contracts among different actors. This contractual nature brings forth the complexity of coercion, complicity and consent.

In this chapter, I examine institutional politics and power forming the neoliberal contract in two principal ways. Methodologically, I explore areas of tension and conflict among stakeholders in the field of women's micro-entrepreneurship—these can be ideological, discursive and practice-related differences, disagreements, gaps and discontents among the stakeholders. These tensions are managed and contained within the field through a complex interplay of coercion and consent, whereby certain actors have the leverage within the institutional power structure to coerce other actors to a certain conduct (i.e., state authority has legal power to require the NGO to provide a specific report). Importantly, I also examine areas lacking tensions and conflicts. To paraphrase Barbra Cruickshank's theoretical statement, lack of resistance must not be mistaken for the lack of politics and power (1999: 5). Areas of consensus, of the taken-for-granted, are achieved and reproduced politically. Coercion and consensus thus constitute the two pillars of analysis, recalling the application of Antonio Gramsci's theory of hegemony in the study of neoliberalism (Plehwe et al., 2006; Howson & Smith, 2008) and even more specifically, in critical entrepreneurship research (Kenny & Scriver, 2012). Gramsci's conceptualisation of hegemony is useful here precisely because it recognises the complex interrelation among coercion and consensus in the way power operates.

Why and how were women's economic empowerment organisations created? If in the global South, women's economic empowerment initiatives have grown in response to top-down approached of development, in the North they have emerged primarily in response to the more recent neoliberal shifts and policies of the state. Civil society initiatives have embarked on micro-entrepreneurship primarily in response to economic needs of marginalised women that the state failed to meet. And, as we shall see, the state could not be compelled to meet those needs through the traditional political claims. Upon establishing the background leading to the re-engagement among civil society, state and market, I turn to investigating the nature of this contract. I trace the ideological, legal-administrative, and bureaucratic mechanisms constituting and regulating the relations among institutions. Moving beyond general and perhaps predictable arguments on the subjection of civil society to neoliberal logic, I analyse and discuss the operation of power through three specific mechanisms of the neoliberal contract identified.

The first mechanism is the structural re-organisation of relations among state, market and civil society. This process blurs the boundaries between them as separate spheres, and reconfigures them in closer relation to each other. Such re-organisation is evident, for instance, in the relatively new practice by which both civil society organisations and commercial companies enter bids and competitions to become contractors of women's economic empowerment projects financed or co-financed by the state. Although this re-division of labour carries some regional and transnational character, it varies significantly among countries, depending on country-specific arrangements of state-civil society relations. Germany and Israel thus present an interesting comparative case of difference in this regard, and so the country-specific consequences for institutional politics are examined.

The second mechanism is the imposition of market-based evaluation logic and practices on civil society organisations. The comprehension of what constitutes success in women's economic empowerment is demonstrated as a form of power over this field and its agents. In the sphere of international development and non-governmental organisations broadly, success and progress are measured and evaluated through various frameworks of Monitoring and Evaluation (M&E). While mainstream Monitoring and Evaluation frameworks claim to be value-neutral and objective sets of scientific and quantitative tools, they are profoundly ideological and political in their power to define what counts as success and progress and which results have value in social and economic change. It is a vivid example of subjection of civil society to neoliberal logic in the interplay between consent and coercion. This observation strongly resonates with recent literature that grasps neoliberalism primarily as extension of market-based evaluation, assessment and judgement measures into non-market domains, including legal, social and cultural spheres (Davies, 2016). In discussing this mechanism and its effect on women's economic empowerment, I also reflect on feminist critical engagement with Monitoring and Evaluation.

The third mechanism is the binary of society and economy, enhanced and sustained by the unquestioned domination of neoclassical economics (discussed in detail in Chap. 4). While social-justice-oriented NGOs attempt to accommodate the "social" in the "economic", they nonetheless continue reproducing them as binary concepts and oppositional spheres, entailing multiple contradictions (Kandlik Eltanani, 2011). The opposition between the economic and the social is thus re-established as an ontological trait central to the field of women's economic empowerment, as it is to the neoliberal order at large. The economic is reduced to and equated with capitalism and ideas of profit maximisation, competition and individualism, while the social is equated with altruism and the common good. The economy in this context hence remains in the grasp of capitalist ideology and neoclassical economics, largely impenetrable to social critique and, as Chap. 4 illustrates, to feminist economics as well.

In the process of their re-engagement, institutions of civil society, state and market re-define each other's ideology and practice. On the one hand, they locate women's micro-entrepreneurship within complex and contradictory ideologies and practices; on the other hand, they gradually reduce and erase these complexities and contradictions through either imposition or complicity with institutional and bureaucratic processes of quality control, funding structures, evaluation measures. These and other means serve to de-politicise the encounter among these institutional actors, and naturalise market-based terms, norms and practices.

I suggest that the consensual and contractual aspect of the field creates a matrix of institutional inter-dependencies, makes invisible conceptual differences among the institutional actors, and forecloses possibilities for frontal resistance and opposition. Indeed, the capacity of capitalism as such for change, its ability to incorporate criticism of its opponents and to accommodate certain mechanisms in order to retain its moral grounds is evident in action. Under those conditions, women's economic empowerment and microfinance organisations are committed and at times able to aid individual marginalised women, while operating within the existing social and economic structures. They do not attempt to provide structural solutions or to tackle core forces that continue marginalising migrant, indigenous and minority women on the national and the global scale. Acknowledging the awareness of many civil society actors of their own limitations, this argument is not intended as an external criticism of their committed, hard and often underpaid work; rather, it aims to explain the structural constraints for civil society organisations to counter economic marginalisation and to realise their aspirations for social and economic justice.

Let us proceed to tracing the emergence of two pioneering organisations that turned to micro-entrepreneurship in order to economically empower marginalised women—the Berlin-based Initiative of Self-Employed Immigrants (*Initiative Selbständiger Immigrantinnen—ISI e.V*) and the Haifa-based Association for Economic Empowerment for Women (*AEEW—העמותה להעצמה כלכלית לנשים ע"ר*). Genealogies of women's economic empowerment and micro-entrepreneurship organisations tell the story of their creation and allow grounding the rationale for their re-engagement with the state and the market in concrete historical and political conditions. These conditions may differ greatly from one national context to another, allowing us to capture the versatility of neoliberal processes across different contexts.

AEEW was established in Israel against the background of the accelerating neoliberal policies of the right-wing government in the late 1990s. In Germany, the background for the establishment of ISI e.V. was the crisis of Fordism and the closing of factories, which has caused many immigrant women to lose their jobs in the late 1980s, as the German Democratic Republic ceased to exist and Germany experienced the turbulence of reunification. AEEW and ISI e.V. grew in different years, under substantially different external conditions, and defined their target audiences slightly differently—low-income women and immigrant women, respectively. Yet, both emerged out of realities of marginalised women's lives and their needs, on the one hand, and the failure of the state to address these realities and needs, on the other hand. Both target women on the margins of citizenship, who are both economically disadvantaged, and belong to an ethnic or national minority (the concrete trajectories of citizenship in each national context are discussed in Chap. 6). What could be perceived as a process of disengaging from the state, at least in the capacity of rights-claiming citizens, has in fact been, as we shall see, a process of re-engagement with the state and the market in a new contract.

AEEW was founded in 1997 (registered in 2000) by women active in Woman to Woman—Haifa Feminist Centre, the oldest Israeli feminist grassroots organisation. AEEW's flagship programme is *A Business of One's Own* (*עסק משלך*)—wordplay on the feminist classic by Virginia Woolf, *A Room of One's Own*—which offers empowerment and business training to low-income women. This programme was inspired by the microfinance model of Muhammad Yunus and the Grameen Bank, and Yunus' book still occupies a central place on AEEW's bookshelf in the reception room. AEEW's establishment was urged by a combination of factors in the country, among them the neoliberal macro-economic shifts in state policy, extensive welfare cutbacks, and increasing attention of feminists to feminisation of poverty, economic injustice and the intersections of gender, ethnicity and class.

Although liberalisation and privatisation of state services began in Israel already in the 1970s, the major ideological shift has occurred during the 1980s and 1990s, fuelled by global neoliberal forces and their eager local proponents. The state was no longer perceived as the driving force of economic and social development: this role has been projected onto the business sector. The policies of a right-wing government have stricken one blow after another to the welfare state, rejecting it as an idea and as a policy. Benjamin Netanyahu, an eager propagator of the free market, in his capacity as the Prime Minister (1996–1999) and later as the Minister of Finance (2003–2005), has conducted far-reaching economic reforms, including privatisation of several state bodies and major cutbacks in welfare and social security. The policy has focused on economic growth, while poverty rates have continued rising significantly. Research has shown that the economic growth was accompanied by increased income of the upper classes, but had little significance for the income of middle and lower classes. These gaps also had a strong ethno-national and gendered character, given that ethno-national and gender-based inequalities in Israel preceded this neoliberal wave. Poverty has been and continued to be the reality for many Palestinian women as well as for Mizrahi and Jewish ultra-Orthodox women.

A veteran AEEW practitioner recalled in her account not only the factual increase in poverty, but also the public atmosphere of the time: "There was a wave of hostility and hatred targeting people in poverty, coming mostly from the United States. It targeted people who receive welfare payments, women and especially single mothers. And the women who were the victims of this hostility, they have internalized it." Another practitioner interpreted the actions of policy-makers to be guided by a "disappearance fantasy", that is, the desire to erase the poor people from public view. Policies at the turn of the millennia included compulsory welfare-to-work programmes for the unemployed, and various penalizing and disciplining systems. The hostility towards the unemployed and those living in poverty is not aimed at all people equally. While in the late 1990s it focused on single mothers, the practitioners I interviewed in the 2010s estimated that it now targets primarily religious ultra-Orthodox families and Palestinian women, as well as older women. The category of "single mothers" is also coloured in the Israeli collective imagination with racialised and ethnic characteristic, referring predominantly to Mizrahi women (Lavie, 2014), and to some extent also to Russian-speaking immigrant women. During the 1990s, feminisation of poverty gained attention and became a theme of interest for women's rights organisations. The increasing awareness of feminists to intersectionality and the questions of ethnicity and class further reinforced this focus. In the Israeli feminist context, this awareness came predominantly because of struggles by Mizrahi feminists within and on the margins of the Israeli feminist movement. Mizrahi women—first, second and later generations of Jews from Middle Eastern and North-African countries—have experienced institutional racism since the establishment of the state, and eventually have placed the intersections of poverty, ethnicity and class on the Israeli feminist agenda (Dahan-Kalev, 2001). I should note already here that the development of Israeli feminism almost entirely takes place within Zionist ideology and denial of Israel's historical and present injustice towards the Palestinian people (Shalhoub-Kevorkian, 2014). This political context comes to the forefront of analysis in Chap. 6; for the purposes of the current discussion, it is enough to note that AEEW develops in an Israeli feminist space embedded in the Israeli national ideology, where Palestinian women with Israeli citizenship are present but recognised as an Arab minority rather than as a colonised Palestinian people. While there are economic empowerment organisations founded by and for Palestinian women in Israel, AEEW exists primarily in the Jewish-Israeli field, albeit at the time of this research, the Executive Director of AEEW was Palestinian, and several programmes targeted Palestinian women.

Following the neoliberal reforms, feminists embarked on agendas for socio-economic justice, and finally concluded that their attempts to counter and halt the accelerating neoliberal policies are failing. The disillusionment was painful. It was clear that the needed support for women facing poverty would not come from the government, which was headed in the exact opposite direction. Ultimately, the realisation that stopping the anti-welfare policies is well beyond their power led feminist activists to found AEEW and to adopt the model of micro-entrepreneurship as a grassroots response to the growing poverty of women.

What is the meaning of giving up on policy change, and turning to grassroots autonomous action? There is a long-standing criticism targeted at civil society and women's rights organisations for substituting the state where it fails to deliver on its obligations to its citizens. However, this story suggests that an autonomous action of the civil society—particularly feminist grassroots groups, as I am not referring to large-scale NGOs here—does not simply come instead of engagement on the political level of lobby and advocacy. It is not a mere complicity with so-called substituting the state, nor a choice of convenience to become "a-political" and to provide services instead of engaging in political struggles. It also cannot be fully explained by the process of NGOisation of the Israeli women's movement and its associated multiplication of social and political strategies. Rather, the choice to shift from policy change to autonomous action evidently came, among other factors, from the painful realisation of civil society activists that acting on the institutional political level to counter neoliberalism leads to a dead end. Feminists turned to micro-entrepreneurship upon encountering the limits of the political system to provide viable means of opposition to neoliberal ideologies, policies and practices of the government. With this considered, it is no longer possible to reduce the establishment of women's micro-entrepreneurship organisations such as AEEW to the de-politicisation and NGOisation of civil society. Rather, it links to a much broader phenomenon of the structural limitations of civil society to block the neoliberal course of economic and social reforms, and simply the sense of activists that they are out of other options.

Feminist initiatives like AEEW are thus not stories of entrepreneurship as a silver bullet or uncritical embrace of market-based solutions to socio-economic problems; rather, it is an action in the absence of satisfactory alternatives and avenues of policy change in neoliberal times. AEEW founders and practitioners are crystal clear that micro-entrepreneurship is only a solution for some women, not all, and is an insufficient measure in ensuring women's access to the labour market and the improvement of their economic status. At the time of research, AEEW was an active member of a coalition of NGOs to lobby and advocate for women's economic rights, evidently refusing to give up completely on the path of policy change, and making some—albeit humble—claims on the state.

At the same time, we should not forget that a key characteristic of women's economic empowerment is the investment in the personal transformation of marginalised women, rather than policy change or other structural changes in social, economic and political systems. The main site of intervention becomes the marginalised woman herself—her way of thinking, acting, being in the world. The logic of empowerment defines her for the resources or powers she lacks (knowledge, confidence, capital), and aims to complement that void through a range of practices. Economic distress is thus understood as an action that marginalised women fail to take or a subject they fail to become. To paraphrase Cruikshank (1999), powerlessness of marginalised populations is positioned as a subjective feeling that can be transformed, and not as an objective reality calling for a transformation in its own right.

ISI e.V. *(Initiative Selbständiger Immigrantinnen e.V.*—Initiative of Self-employed Immigrants) was founded in Berlin in 1988 and officially registered in 1991. The initiative has emerged out of a UNESCO Conference on Women and International Migration, which took place at the Technical University of Berlin. In this conference, the participants learned of entrepreneurship development projects in the United Kingdom and France, and recognised its potential as a solution for the unemployed immigrant women in Berlin. The project was ultimately designed after a model of Women's Enterprise Development Agency in Birmingham, UK. A co-founder of the organisation described: "[I]n 88–89 we started the organisation ISI because of the high unemployment rates of women guest workers in the industry. And it is not the issue that women did not want to work, which in the 90s and 2000s has been reflected upon this group of women. But just the opposite, these women wanted to work, but they had become unemployed and they were not getting the access to re-education for better jobs."

This description mirrors the circumstances for the emergence of AEEW, and recalls the narrative of public hostility toward racialised groups of women and the rhetoric of "not willing to work". Public hostility and blaming-and-shaming rhetoric towards the poor and the unemployed is well familiar across national contexts. If in neoliberalism a person is responsible for their own employment, well-being and happiness, they are also responsible for their own unemployment, exclusion and misery. The other side of the glorified entrepreneur is the abject and hated unemployed person, who is racialised, class-based and gendered. And, as with the Israeli case, this widespread belief that immigrant women "do not want to work" has made policy change a more difficult task. ISI e.V. founders were of course deeply critical of this perception, stressing that the main problem was the scarcity of employment opportunities for immigrant women, rather than their own lack of motivation.

The collapse of the German Democratic Republic and the re-unification of Germany have fundamentally changed the social and economic conditions for the people in Germany, with the impacts differentiated by East/West division and by factors of gender and migration status, with migration largely standing for race and ethnicity as well as class. The co-founders of ISI e.V. have understood the social, economic and political consequences of the re-unification of Germany for the migrant women in Berlin, and the need to address women's economic needs in new ways. At the same time, Birmingham provided not only an inspiration, but an exemplary case that could be articulated in free-market terms of entrepreneurship promotion, allowing for engagement with policy-makers and securing funds (Ülker, 2012).

In the earlier years, dominated by mass-production and extensive industrial labour, the Federal Republic of Germany has imported labour force from Italy, Greece, Turkey, Morocco, Portugal, Tunisia and Yugoslavia, since mid-1950s until the 1970s. The political rationale of receiving "guest workers" who were expected to work and return to their home countries, ultimately had to come under scrutiny. It became clear that the "guests" and their families have lived in the country for decades, and were not going anywhere. The economic transformation and the declining demand for industrial labour brought about large-scale unemployment. This has brought to surface the issues of immigrants' unemployment and social marginalisation as a pressing problem for Germany. Ülker (2012) draws on these conditions as the context for the rise of the "ethnic entrepreneur", which became one possible way of dealing with large-scale unemployment and its related social distress. Although the majority of the immigrants who had lost their employment were men, and the gendered construction of the "ethnic entrepreneur" assumed a masculine identity, immigrant women similarly lost their jobs after the closing of factories and the reforms brought by the reunification. The establishment of ISI e.V. therefore takes place in the context of women's pressing economic needs, in the lack of adequate solutions by the state and in the appeal of entrepreneurship solutions to civil society and state authorities alike.

This brief contextualisation of the emergence of women's economic empowerment and micro-entrepreneurship organisations sets the stage for a new contract among civil society, state and market. In a comparative perspective, the turn of German and Israeli civil society organisations to micro-entrepreneurship initiatives for marginalised women is both rooted in distinct economic-political contexts and points to global and transnational trends. Both cases draw on inspiration and examples from other regions and countries: Muhammad Yunus for AEEW and the Birmingham example for ISI e.V. Both stories speak to the limited capacity of citizens to advocate for policies contradicting the neoliberal spirit and to find solutions to poverty, unemployment and labour market discrimination within the political sphere that is between citizens and the state. Finally, the drive of the activists and founders of initiatives like AEEW and ISI e.V. testify to the motivation of civil society to take responsibility, to create and develop solutions to social and economic problems unmet by the state and aggravated by its neoliberal course. Importantly, this was not simply a naïve turn for the civil society, but rather seeing an absence of available alternatives for marginalised women to survive in the changing economy. AEEW and ISI e.V., as many other feminist or women-led organisations in the field, recognise the partiality of entrepreneurship as a solution, and acknowledge that broader interventions on policy level are required in order to advance women's economic rights and independence. To this end, NGOs do establish collaborations and larger civil society and engage with policymakers, beyond the concrete sphere of WEE and micro-entrepreneurship that is the focus of their work.

We see that civil society and feminist activists chose to deal with the unemployment and poverty of marginalised women outside of the traditional political sphere vis-à-vis the state: they were no longer claiming policy solutions from the state in their capacity as citizens, at least not as their primary path of action. Instead, they re-engaged with the state in other ways. The most obvious form of re-engagement is administrative. As NGOs enter the public domain of legitimacy, they must legally register in order to be able to perform basic economic functions: to receive funding, to hire staff, to make payments to service providers. Official registration means developing an administrative and bureaucratic relationship with state authorities, and subjecting the organisation to their regulation. The receipt of funding means immediate engagement in institutional relationships with financing bodies, public or private, and hence negotiations on priorities, content, ways of working and more. Funding often comes with a predetermined framework in terms of time, scope and content priorities, to which the NGOs have to adjust and accommodate themselves, if they wish to be eligible for that funding. Simply put, funding comes with strings attached, although the nature of these strings may vary among funders and funding schemes. The dependency on funding makes NGOs vulnerable to various pressures from their current and potential funders. In principle, NGOs are free to engage with funders of their choice. In practice, there are similarities in the standard demands made by donors, and the decision to engage (or not) with a donor is made under conditions of constant financial pressure. This pressure is increased if the NGO employs personnel and is committed to providing job security to people depending on it for their livelihoods. We already begin to see a complex interplay between coercion and consent.

Both Germany and Israel are members of the intergovernmental economic organisation OECD (Organisation for Economic Co-operation and Development), Israel since 2010, West Germany as a founding member, and of course are not on the receiving end of international development financial aid. In the global South, much of women's economic empowerment and microfinance programmes come from international development funds, which is already one major difference between Northern and Southern economic empowerment fields—the financing architecture. Civil society funding structures differ substantially between Germany and Israel. Generally, the NGO world is characterised by financial insecurity and instability, due to factors like limited period of funding cycles: many donors make grants on an annual basis, so that most small and medium-sized NGOs are constantly insecure about their funding from one year to the next. In some countries, like Germany, civil society heavily relies on state funding, which may be multi-year and places its recipients in a rather privileged position; in others, like Israel, they must seek out foreign sources of funding, often on a year-by-year basis. The intervention of funding institutions in the ideology, discourse and practice of civil society organisations functions in direct and often indirect forms. Power relations among NGOs and donors are overt, and often disguised under the rhetoric of partnership. I should note that funding in itself is both a heterogeneous and dynamic field—feminist and other progressive funds are pioneering transformative and power-aware forms of engagement and advocate for more feminist funding policies and practices. I am referring here specifically to the funding landscape for women's economic empowerment, which is also naturally not without exceptions, and, in case of OECD countries non-eligible for development aid, it is also quite country-specific.

While most funders are not involved in the daily implementation of projects, their involvement is evident in other ways, such as their requirements for Monitoring and Evaluation. These assessments heavily influence the organisational culture, discourse and practices of civil society. Another feature of the field is that donors' priorities often depend on trends, so that different social causes are fashionable in different times. I have encountered women's rights organisations in Israel refused funding by donors who were interested primarily in women's economic empowerment at that time; meanwhile, the cause has lost its fashionable moment and the NGOs in the sphere of economic empowerment struggle for funding once again. One AEEW practitioner expressed a critical position on this state of affairs: "I often say, we have to amuse them [the foundations] in a way. If you don't amuse them, they are bored [...] It is often with foundations, that instead of strengthening what we have, they want something new. Now, this something new... sometimes they even want a new NGO. But bottom line, once you get the money, they intervene less." The funders' expectation or demand for short-term innovations does not correlate with the long-term approach to social and economic change that many civil society organisations in this field embrace. Indeed, feminist organisations and women's funds have long advocated for core, multi-year flexible funding for long-term transformative social change rather than shorter-term project-based funding. Yet, as long as NGOs must amuse the funders, the amusement can take, for example, the form of repackaging old activities and projects under new names when possible, or actually variating in activities, even though the actual priority might be to "strengthen what we have". Civil society organisations consent to engage in this interaction, ultimately in order to get the funding they need.

State and municipal authorities can also be the funders, and thus partake in women's micro-entrepreneurship in a number of capacities. They are the regulators of entrepreneurship-related legal and administrative conditions, but can also be project initiators contracting civil society organisations and/or commercial companies to implement entrepreneurship training projects, or, partners in a project initiated by a civil society organisation, either by becoming a direct funder or through other means, for example, providing meeting rooms or logistical support. State laws regulate civil society organisations with regard to loans provision: with few exceptions, loans must go through designated banks, microfinance institutions, and other financial institutions. For example, few years into its activity, AEEW had to give up on the provision of micro-credit to its beneficiaries in order to become eligible for tax-free donations in Israel (beforehand they were eligible for tax-free donations from abroad, and taxed donations in Israel). This decision was not taken easily or unanimously in the organisation. AEEW staff and Board largely rejected the idea that microfinancing bodies should not be entitled to tax-free donations in the country. This points to an initial conflict in the perception of microfinancing between the NGO—which perceived microfinancing as central to its non-profit activities, and the state—which perceives taxation appropriate for microfinance, understanding it as essentially profit-making activity, subjected to market logic. In this case, like in many others, the conflict was settled in favour of the latter, in the spirit of commercialisation of social economy—in this case, with the state as an agent of commercialisation. This compromise demonstrates the structural dependence of civil society organisations on legal-administrative regulations and on the profit-oriented economic and financial logic behind them—the same logic civil society organisations set out to confront. The arrangement by which civil society organisations operate on state funding is also an ambivalent one, in terms of its political implications. If civil society organisations provide citizens with services and thereby address needs that the state fails to meet, having the costs covered by tax money appears as a reasonable arrangement. On the other hand, in this arrangement, civil society becomes in effect a contractor of the state. If civil society organisations operate as contractors of the state, to what extent can civil society be perceived as a potential counter-force, as a factor of accountability, or as an alternative logic for social and economic justice?

The brief but dense history of Mikrokreditfonds Deutschland demonstrates the complexities of engagement between state, market and civil society, within the field of microfinance, and the sometimes-unexpected re-organisation of roles among them. Mikrokreditfonds Deutschland is a microfinancing scheme, which began in 2000 as a pilot of the GLS bank and NGOs in Berlin-Brandenburg, under the name GLS Mikrofinanzfonds (microfinance funds). These NGOs functioned as microfinancing institutions, responsible for managing the contact with the beneficiaries. In 2004, the federal government entered the project and expanded it to the federal level, with the aim to improve access to capital for micro-enterprises and start-ups in Germany. In 2014, the fund already had a volume of €100 million from the federal budget and from the European Social Fund.

The entrance of state authorities into the programme generated far-reaching and profound transformations in the design of the funding scheme and in the relations among the actors involved. These transformations illuminate the multifaceted role of the state in the field. The Ministry of Labour and Social Affairs (Bundesministerium für Arbeit und Soziales: BMAS) and the Federal Ministry for Economic Affairs and Energy (Bundesministerium für Wirtschaft und Energie: BMWi) brought in large budgets, and the number of microfinancing institutions grew rapidly from about 10 in its early years, to 35 in 2009–2010. This sharp growth has fundamentally changed the relations among the bank and the microfinance institutions. In an interview, an employee of the bank has described to me, not without nostalgia, the close relations and a sense of solidarity among the GLS bank and the microfinance institutions in the era of GLS Mikrofinanzfonds. The increase of funds was accompanied by bureaucratisation and standardisation of the process, assigning the bank a narrow bureaucratic role of coordinating the funds. Some of the new microfinance institutions failed to function well, to provide credible recommendations and to manage the loans properly. The interpersonal contact and the relations of trust among the bank and the microfinance institutions were lost. The state did not, however, simply replace the bank, re-assuming responsibility for the provision of economic opportunities to its citizens. Together with the funds, the state brought into the project the demand for profitability. The fact that the requirement for profitability came from the state rather than the bank is somewhat ironic. Co-founding the programme, the bank perceived it to be part of its social engagement practices, deviating to an extent from its main economic activities and an exception to its logic of profitability. The bank's initial deviation from the logic of profitability was enabled in the first place by an ontological split among the economic and the social—a split that is being increasingly challenged by the subordination all forms of social economy to the logic of market economy (Berkovitch & Kemp, 2010). This is not always a clear-cut top-down dynamic. One mechanism driving this subordination for civil society organisations is the aspiration for sustainability. This aspiration comes not only from donors in the form of conditions and demands, but also from NGOs themselves, as they wish to reduce dependency on donors and external funding. Mikrokreditfonds Deutschland is thus an example of a new hybrid of the state, civil society and the market. The entrance of the state shifted the role of the bank from that of a partner in a social project, to that of a contractor of the state in a social-commercial project. The process has disciplined the bank back into its role, and the state assumed ownership for the project in a double form: taking responsibility for its citizens' economic well-being, while further subjecting this economic well-being to market logics and to the capacities of the individual citizen even further—in a more bureaucratised process and at higher interest rates.

State funding for NGOs is a global phenomenon, yet it differs greatly among countries. The difference between civil society in Germany and Israel is a good example. In Germany, civil society organisations often receive a lion's share of their funding from authorities on municipal, state or federal levels, or from EU institutions like the ESF, which essentially can also be seen as a form of state funding. This is indeed the case for ISI e.V. and other German NGOs focused on women's economic empowerment, from entrepreneurship training and networking (like WeiberWirtschaft eG.) to the provision of micro-credit (like Goldrausch e.V.). State funding for these organisations is often fixed for several years, providing a relative level of stability. In stark contrast, civil society in Israel generally does not enjoy extensive municipal or state funding. NGOs like AEEW raise the majority of their funds from private foundations, primarily U.S.-based Jewish foundations.

Practitioners from both German and Israeli NGOs expressed the position that the state should in fact fund them. Israeli practitioners argued that instead of creating new models of economic empowerment, the state should actively support existing models practiced by grassroots organisations possessing the most relevant experience and expertise. However, Israeli state authorities do not express any particular need or interest in active cooperation with civil society. Grassroots organisations are often disregarded, if not viewed as a nuisance. The more formal and institutionalised associations in the economic sphere, such as industry unions and commerce chambers, are acknowledged by the state as an important source of information and consultation about the needs of their constituencies. In an interview with an official of the Authority for Small and Medium Businesses in the Ministry of Economy, I confirmed that beyond polite formalities of "welcoming" the existence of grassroots NGOs, there is no interest to allocate them funding as a form of state support. A practitioner shared: "[O]nce we were in the Ministry of Trade and Commerce, and we go there because we want budgets. They told us clearly, we don't want too many NGOs, we don't want NGOs at all. Why do we need to support NGOs? Why? It is easier to us, we have the MATIs—it is also an NGO, but it is somehow, they are somehow connected, they receive budgets from the Ministry, it is better that for them that it will be like that." By and large, civil society organisations—particularly grassroots NGOs—are less desired by the Israeli state authorities as either contractors for projects or as partners in policy-related dialogue, certainly in comparison to European standards. The Israeli Authority for Small and Medium Businesses preferred to create MATI (today: MAOF), its own network of organisations specialising in entrepreneurship advancement, and most recently to re-structure them to be under complete control of the Authority. It is worth noting that while GNGOs, governmental non-governmental organisations, are mostly associated with undemocratic and totalitarian regimes, the European Union (EU) also regularly launches initiatives formally defined as civil society and as non-governmental, making the division between state and non-state actors less than clear. Civil society organisations are clearly unsatisfied with this situation, and as mentioned before, believe they should be funded by the state.

The lack of state funds appears to have some positive, if unintended, consequences. It is true that NGOs not financed by the state have to invest extensive efforts and resources in fundraising (managing ten or twenty donors rather than one or two), and that the lack of multi-year stable funding undermines long-term planning and engagement in long-term activities. Yet, the need to raise funds from a variety of non-state donors, and to "amuse" them, also allows NGOs to pursue a variety of priorities and activities. To illustrate, AEEW has launched a saving programme as well as so-called incubators to support women entrepreneurs after securing designated funds for them from various sources—an activity ISI e.V. would like to engage in, but is beyond its centralised funding agreement with the ESF. Furthermore, some of the smaller donors can be more open to changes and negotiations than others, and certainly more than highly bureaucratised institution such as German federal ministries or the ESF. As contractors of the state, German NGOs cannot pursue directions of activity that are outside the scope of predefined state priorities. In short, it provides a greater degree of freedom in areas of action. Nonetheless, it is hard to underestimate the constant financial uncertainty, which prevents the realisation of these possibilities.

Civil society organisations are not the sole competitors for state tenders for women's empowerment and micro-entrepreneurship projects.

Commercial companies increasingly enter competition with civil society organisations, blurring the distinctions among these actors: both become contractors for state- initiated and sponsored projects. This conduct is institutionalised in Germany, and recently begun taking place in Israel, much to the understandable dissatisfaction of the NGOs. When state authorities issue tenders for social causes, they effectively turn these causes into potentially profitable spheres, and thus attract commercial profit-oriented companies. Women's economic empowerment ceases to be a solely ideologically motivated cause, and becomes a potentially profitable business venture. Israeli NGOs have critically pointed to situations bordering absurdity from their point of view, when a company specialising in audio products won a tender to conduct women's empowerment courses. As a result, the implementation of these activities becomes disconnected from any feminist ideologies and visions of social transformation and economic justice. Berkovich and Kemp (2010) discuss this as part of a larger phenomenon, as social economy is increasingly embraced by international financial institutions and state authorities, while undergoing commercialisation and subjection to market discourses and practices.

The case of "Gleichstellen for the Equality of Women in the Economy" illustrates the invisible power of the funding framework (in this case the ESF) to shape the substance and limitations of economic empowerment programmes. Gleichstellen (literally "to make equal") is a German federal programme launched to advance the equality of women in the economy. Gleichstellen was created by the German Federal Ministry of Labour and Social Affairs. Funded primarily by the ESF, it brings together employers' associations, trade unions, commercial companies and civil society organisations. These institutional actors are not unanimous in their understanding of gender inequality, its root causes and, subsequently, appropriate intervention strategies. Their differences became evident throughout the planning committee meetings, resulting in ongoing disagreements, stormy discussions and attempts to reach agreements on various accounts. Yet, as I have learned in an interview, the core political issue—the main thematic areas of the programme—was never even discussed, because these themes were set in advance by the ESF. A political discussion on the causes of and remedies to economic inequality from a gender perspective simply never took place in this encounter among state, civil society and market institutions. This can explain why only one out of about 150 projects to advance women's equality in the economy has explicitly addressed immigrant women, although they are among the most socio-economically marginalised populations in Germany. This case serves well to illustrate the de-politicisation of such encounters, as the neoliberal approach moves social affairs from the political and argumentative to the contractual and bureaucratic (Davies, 2016).

Women's economic empowerment, as these examples show, is a field characterised by structural re-organisation of relations among state, market and civil society. This re-organisation produces hybrids as well as institutional engagements that effectively prevent political confrontation, even among actors with seemingly contradicting ideologies and priorities. We also see that the funding body has major power over the discourse and practices of civil society, as the case with ESF and Gleichstellen, dictating the thematic substantive boundaries of what constitutes the advancement of gender equality in the economy. Definition of target groups, with the current example of absence of immigrant women, is one illustration. The influence of the EU on women's micro-entrepreneurship extends beyond its borders. Although Israel is not an EU Member State, the EU and Israel have an extensive Association Agreement concerning economic and other forms of cooperation. The European Commission's Delegation to Israel is a significant funder for civil society in Israel. The considerable size of EU grants (reaching amounts as €300,000) turns the EU into one of the most desirable funders for civil society organisations in Israel, particularly progressive NGOs in areas of peace-building, human rights and gender equality. The EU has been financing some projects women's economic empowerment and entrepreneurship training, for instance the grassroots organisation of Arab women in the city of Jaffa *Arous El-Bahar*, although this support was not major or significant over the years and has taken place in the framework of EU's Partnership for Peace programme. As a close economic partner of the EU and as a relatively fresh member of OECD (since September 10th, 2010), Israel is increasingly evaluated by European standards. These standards exercise productive power, in that they influence the course of action of the state. Various EU assessments are intended to discipline a state into proper conduct according to the standards set by the EU, in a process of standardisation. The following excerpt from an interview with a representative of the Israeli Ministry of Economy demonstrates this point: "As far as the Israeli government is concerned, there is no governmental policy to take care of women entrepreneurs. It is not a theme defined as a priority for a specific policy. And that is indeed one of the points of criticism that we have received from the EU in their assessment of the Israeli policy of support for small and medium businesses according to the SBA." While Israeli civil servants can be sceptical of EU's standards and are in no hurry to comply, ultimately these models do have an influence. For instance, EU's insistence on gender, and Israel's low scores on that, may motivate the Authority for SMBs or individual civil servants within it to push for gender mainstreaming. Of course, explicit commitment to gender equality is insufficient for its actual advancement and implementation as scholars note for the EU institutions themselves (Weiner & MacRae, 2014).

The second pillar of the neoliberal contract is the market-based evaluation logic. Monitoring and Evaluation is a framework of practice by which NGOs are required to measure their impact and whether they are meeting their objectives and achieving their intended results. For NGOs worldwide, Monitoring and Evaluation has become part of the taken-for-granted, of common sense. And indeed, at a first glance Monitoring and Evaluation makes sense. The trend for "more monitoring and evaluation" and more quantifiable results and evidence of impact is a global one, spanning across all spheres and sectors of civil society and beyond (Batliwala & Pittman, 2010). This is an institutional chain of pressure, as many donors, themselves recipients of grants, must in turn present their own donors with quantifiable results. If their donors are governments, evaluation requirements are as a rule included in their contracts, and then passed on to the grantee NGOs. If their donors are individuals, the NGO may be urged to show results not by written contracts, but by the need to compete with other organisations and present tangible results and compelling publications and reports to gain an advantage and become more attractive to funders.

Overall, this trend presents less of a problem for development, aid and relief agencies, which are able to easily present quantifiable evidence of their work, such as distributing X food parcels to Y people, delivering X medicine to Y hospitals, and so on. It does, however, present a major problem for NGOs concerned with long-term social and economic change and with transformation of attitudes, values and beliefs in society, where impact cannot be easily measured (Garbutt, 2013). Social realities and processes are complex, non-linear, full of setbacks and backlashes, and involve a great number of factors. With regard to entrepreneurship for example, it has been noted for micro-enterprises of women and immigrants that the business often remains for a long time in-between success and failure (Bührmann & Pongratz, 2010). This makes quantifiable evidence a challenging and problematic task, and creates an in-built tension among the NGOs and their donors, as a practitioner has explained: "Look, the impression is that the donors want results in numbers. They can claim otherwise, and say that they want to hear personal stories too, but at the end of the day, they want to see the statistics and the numbers. How many businesses opened, how many registered, what was the income, how did the income increase from one year to the next. So there's always this thing—tell us a personal story, and how great it is, but eventually…".

The planning, monitoring and evaluation of projects are presented as both a science and an art. There is an entire industry of Monitoring and Evaluation experts and consulting firms, complex spreadsheets and manuals to read, workshops and courses for NGO practitioners, conferences and certified studies. Yet, these are not merely technical tools and tasks to master, but rather ways of thinking, judging and assessing reality, an undoubtedly ideological and political realm. Interestingly, some of the most popular Monitoring and Evaluation frameworks have their origins in military and corporate spheres, hinting at some of their ideological and political underpinnings. Consider for example the Logical Framework Approach (LFA)—a standard and widely used instrument for planning, designing, monitoring and evaluating projects. It is adopted and required by many international development agencies, including the inland and overseas funding schemes of the EU. Although popular information sources such as Wikipedia trace the LFA to the US International Development Agency, it in fact originates in the US military and later US space agency NASA (Bakewell & Garbutt, 2005). We thus see penetration of military and corporate logics into civil society, and their role in setting the standards of what is logical, and how progress and success can be measured (Davies, 2016). A comprehensive study on LFA's advantages and disadvantages has found that despite its many problems, the LFA is tolerated by both donors and NGOs because "it imposes a uniform way of thinking with a formal way of recording project or programme work and a common presentation that everyone who has been initiated into the LFA can read and understand. It makes their job easier" (Bakewell & Garbutt, 2005:18). This is precisely the political impact of Monitoring and Evaluation: it introduces a common language and a uniform way of thinking into civil society globally, thereby making a seemingly technical monitoring and evaluation of projects into a process of ideological standardisation. The evaluation logic of a women's economic empowerment project thus might end up looking not very different from a military strategy or at the very least a corporate marketing plan.

It is not surprising that feminist and women's rights organisations, used to working in hostile patriarchal and conservative contexts worldwide, have been critical of the standard Monitoring and Evaluation approaches and its applicability to the real world. They have challenged the existing Monitoring and Evaluation instruments for failing to capture the complexity of women's realities and of feminist social change. Feminist organisations like AWID (Association for Women's Rights in Development) have facilitated the development of alternative, feminist Monitoring and Evaluation tools that are rooted in women's lived realities and in their own perception of success. For instance, a feminist approach to Monitoring and Evaluation points out that success is not only about improving the situation for women. When reactionary forces are strong, stopping the existing situation from deteriorating and keeping the achievements already won (such as the right for a safe abortion)—is in itself an achievement, so that "holding the line" qualifies as a success. AWID's efforts targeted not only NGOs, but also donors, aiming to educate and influence them, and its publication with Monitoring & Evaluation insights for women's organisations is matched with a parallel publication for donors. Feminists have largely accepted that assessment of social change is in itself positive, but have criticised the existing instruments and have been pushing for alternative ones. However, this acceptance is not entirely voluntary. In the current funding structure, NGOs simply have no choice but to agree to the assessment required by the donor, in order to qualify for funding, even if they may have some freedom to negotiate the form and tools of this assessment. The question asked by the critical voices in Monitoring and Evaluation—is Monitoring and Evaluation necessarily a good thing?—is rhetorical and remains open, as it is immediately followed by practical instructions and suggestions on how to better conduct Monitoring and Evaluation, not whether to conduct it. Nonetheless, recent feminist development-related research insists on questioning the imposition of logical framework on women's rights organisations, and advocates for "investment in their capacity to respond creatively to emerging opportunities, more trust in their knowledge, and sensitive, supportive accompaniment" (Cornwall, 2014: 25). These demands challenge the common sense of Monitoring and Evaluation as an inherently good thing, thus shifting the discourse in direction of "trust" and "accompaniment", away from oversight, control, and evaluation of meeting fixed goals and expectations as per military and corporate logics. So far such critical approach dwells on the margins rather than the centre.

I have identified two principal axes of Monitoring and Evaluation related tension among women's micro-entrepreneurship NGOs and their funders: the definition of success and the external assessments of NGOs. These axes of tension make visible the penetration of market-based evaluation logics, practices, and institutions into the sphere of civil society and philanthropy in particular (Edwards, 2008; Somers, 2008; Davies, 2016). The definition of success is a strong point of tension in the field of women's micro-entrepreneurship and microcredit. What makes a project successful, and how is success measured? The power over the setting of goals and objectives for the desired change is a political power over the creation of meanings and the perception of reality. It is also political in the narrower sense of institutional politics in the field: the ability of a project to prove successful can determine its future funding and survival, and by extent the survival of the NGO. However, within the Monitoring and Evaluation framework and discourse, the definition of "success" is not perceived as political, but rather as value-neutral, objective and nearly scientific, and is therefore difficult to challenge. While NGOs are clearly not satisfied with the prevailing evaluation criteria and particularly its quantitative trend, and at times make concrete attempts to engage the donor in altering them, they largely tend to accept it.

Evaluation criteria reveal hierarchical power relations that are often discursively concealed in the NGO and donor world through terms of cooperation and partnership. Ultimately, these criteria are set by donors, and NGOs must relate to them in order to justify their funding and be eligible to re-apply for it. This does not mean that the relations are necessarily one-sided, that there are no co-dependencies, or that NGOs cannot influence the donors to change the evaluation criteria. There is a high degree of diversity among donors; and the more progressive and feminist funders see value in designing evaluation criteria in sincere dialogue with the NGOs they fund. Meanwhile, the instalment of predefined Monitoring and Evaluation procedures means that this space for dialogue is shrinking in favour of the easily quantifiable, quicker and standard criteria setting and evaluation measures. The NGOs themselves, with their limited resources and capacities, also have an interest to meet the requirements as painlessly as possible to get on with their work, and are rarely motivated to engage in long dialogues to revolutionise Monitoring and Evaluation.

To illustrate, for ESF as for other key funders, success is measured by fixed quantitative data, perceived as hard facts. It is about numbers, about the percentage of women replaying loans, opening businesses, or, in some cases, increasing their income. In contrast, grassroots and feminist organisations tend to have a more qualitative, broader and holistic view on what constitutes success. In their perception, it is also a success when a woman hasn't opened a business yet, but was empowered enough through the programme to decide to leave an abusive husband. It is a success if she gained self-confidence and found a job as an employee, rather than opening her business. It is a success if a woman has a realistic and promising business plan, but still struggles to secure financing for it by the end of the project period. A practitioner explained: "ESF has pretty clear criteria, if we are Existenzgründung [starting a micro-enterprise] then we need this statistic, and if our women found employment, then we haven't reached our goal. They found work—we have to throw them out of statistic [...] The criteria need to change. We cannot guarantee that if the women will go to the bank, they will immediately get funding. They created business plans, they learned a lot, they are ready, and now they have to fight for financing, and this is not taken into account. This means they are not selbstständig [self-employed], and are thrown out of statistics."

We thus see a difference in world view and approach among feminist and women's rights organisations and the major financing institutions setting bureaucratic guidelines. While entrepreneurship training is the focus of organisations like ISI e.V., entrepreneurship is ultimately seen as a means of helping women to achieve economic independence, not an end to itself. Hence, if entrepreneurship training has helped a woman to find work as employee instead of opening an enterprise, they would not perceive it as a failure, although they are well aware that for their funders this is not the case. Similarly, they would not address a woman's difficulty to secure financing as her personal failure or their own failure, explaining it instead with external difficulties of the market. When asked about their aspirations and dreams, ISI e.V. employee mentioned that they would also like to expand to providing financial education and training so that women could work as employees in the spheres of accounting and bookkeeping. However, becoming a partner of the state's employment agencies is an expensive endeavour they could not afford embarking on at the time. Moreover, the competition for funds among NGOs requires them to specialise in narrow areas of activity, making broader and holistic approaches to social and economic change more difficult to adopt.

The divergence in the understanding of what constitutes a success reveals in fact a divergence in understanding the socio-economic problems at hand, their root causes and their solutions. While some output is considered success by NGOs rather than by funders, other output is considered success by the funders, but not by the NGOs. A powerful example of that are the criteria of opening a business as an indicator of success. For funders, a micro-enterprise is included in statistics of success. However, for NGOs working closely with women and accompanying their everyday struggles to operate a business, this is far from enough. As Bührmann and Pongratz note (2010), the traditional entrepreneurial discourse of success is less relevant for most micro-entrepreneurs from marginalised backgrounds, because their enterprise is often found between failure and success as a nearly permanent condition. Speaking of their dreams in ISI e.V., a staff member described that they would like to create a service centre for women and to offer financial and legal consulting, but this activity is not funded by the kind of funding they currently have access to. Their funding enables them to offer consulting for the period of one year, but the actual need is far greater.

KIEDF, Israel's main microfinancing institution, encountered a similar situation. Based on their experience, they have realised that a loan repayment is not a good enough indicator of the person actually operating a successful business and improving their financial situation. Even though some level of entrepreneurship training is required for a person to be entitled for a loan, additional business consulting is often needed. However, providing more training and consulting for their clients, would mean scoring less in the prevailing evaluation criteria, namely the number of clients per staff member per year. The practitioner explained that while in Bangladesh and India it can be 500 clients per year, in high-income countries the numbers are between 200 and 500. When KIEDF decided to prioritise support for business development, their staff had less time to manage loans, and they reduced their target to 100. As this interview with a KIEDF employee illustrates, a clash of different perceptions of success can in essence be a clash of different logics: "[T]he clash is that the consideration is to provide a quality product that is not necessarily economic. That is, if we want it to be more economic, meaning more profitable or at least covering our operation costs, because we really are not profitable, we don't even get there… so, the ideology overcame the numbers of our accounting". It is interesting to note that the term economic is used as a synonym for profitable. Economic logic means by default free market, capitalist logic, prioritising profit as the principal goal and meaning of the economic sphere, which is then discursively constructed as inherently distinct from and oppositional to social, society-oriented logic. This contrast between economy and society is characteristic of the women's economic empowerment and micro-entrepreneurship field (Kandlik Eltanani, 2011). Indeed, the possibility of KIEDF to make a choice in favour of their clients rather than to score better in widely accepted evaluation criteria is not self-evident. It was enabled by several factors, such as them being innovators in the field, the first and main microfinancing body in the country, and their reliance on funders many of whom are not experts in microfinance, and therefore do not hold KIEDF accountable according to such criteria. These are rather exceptional conditions; nonetheless, they point out to creative pathways civil society organisations can sometimes find within the existing restraints.

A relatively recent phenomenon of the Monitoring and Evaluation culture is the entrance of actors specialising in rating NGOs and granting them various certificates. This adds to the donors' demand from the NGO to demonstrate effectiveness (predominantly in the sense of cost-effectiveness) in order to compete for funds. A rating by a certain institution is sometimes a condition to apply for funds. Evaluation in itself is not new, nor is the concept of external evaluation; the innovation is in the rating of NGOs by a self-appointed authority, under the active endorsement of donors. Monitoring and Evaluation and quality control can be seen as an industry made of both non-profit and for-profit companies that are designing the standards for NGOs, including social change NGOs. These companies enjoy the legitimacy to rate NGOs and social change, and this rating is increasingly required by public bodies as a proof of the NGO's impact or (cost-) effectiveness.

In Israel, AEEW was tested and rated by Midot Institute, a non-profit organisation established in 2008, with the stated mission of promoting "effectiveness and impact as the main criterion for social investors and for NPO [non-profit organisation] leaders by rating NPOs and producing sector analysis reports". Midot's mission statement reads: "Funders no longer make do with existing reporting standards and are insisting on hard evidence for success and results as a condition for their continued support. Midot was founded in 2008 in response to these trends." Midot was established in order to influence what future distribution of resources in the civil society in Israel, what gets funded and what doesn't. Funders insist on hard evidence and Midot is there to provide it, with their evidence based on (cost-) effectiveness. It has been noted that one side of globalisation in neoliberal times is that of standardisation: of ideas, of problem analysis and of solutions. Donors can request Midot's rating, instead of engaging in in-depth or nuanced discussions with NGOs on what is the meaning of success in their area of social change, in the lives of the people the NGO serves. Indeed, many of them do. This is a strong example of market logic being imposed on the civil society from above, through the structural dependency of civil society organisations on funding. Although formally Midot is registered as a non-profit organisation, it is far from the popular image of a social change association established by concerned citizens or social activists. Midot was established by two powerful institutions, JDC—American Jewish Joint Distribution Committee and Metav Investment House—which in 2012 merged with Dash Investment House, firing 200 employees in the process. Hence, this attempt to re-organise the rules of the game and influence the future for civil society in Israel is coming from an international Jewish organisation and a commercial investment company. De-facto these actors wage substantial power over the entire civil society in Israel and its future. The possibility to score high on this and other similar ratings significantly depends on the resources of each civil society organisation, their human capital and their level of proficiency in the relevant professional terminology. NGOs of middle-class educated professionals with privileged members are likely to score higher than working-class activists and underprivileged communities, whose impactful and meaningful work may not fall into recognised formats of planning, monitoring and evaluation of projects. This process pushes out activists by pressing NGOs to replace grassroots activists and people of lower education levels, with professionals proficient in development discourses, responding to the need to professionalise in order to be eligible for funding. We thus see the dynamics of the NGO world replicating unequal division of resources, rather than challenging it.

In conclusion, tracing the institutional power relations between state, civil society and market in the field of women's micro-entrepreneurship reveals not a self-evident neoliberal story or a simple narrative of the triumph of market ideologies over transformative social agendas. Instead, I have shown and discussed a number of ongoing processes by which neoliberal hegemony is re-established through coercion as well as consent, and specifically through a set of repeated compromises of the civil society in its engagements with the state and the market. In theory, this opens a path for change and contestation of the neoliberal hegemony: civil society organisations could resist compromise, withdraw consent and stop collaboration. In practice, this is very difficult to achieve, taking into account the contractual form that privileges consent and compromise over conflict and confrontation, especially among unequal positions and relations of dependency such as funding. This challenge is compounded by the neoliberal resort to scientific and seemingly neutral and technical discourses and frameworks (such as Monitoring and Evaluation) and the market's capacities for adaptation and co-optation of critical, social and economic justice oriented discourses and practices.

We have also seen how the institutions of civil society, state and market re-define each other's ideologies and practice. On the one hand, they locate women's micro-entrepreneurship within complex and contradictory ideologies and practices, and on the other gradually reduce and erase these complexities and contradictions. This is done primarily through the formalisation of contractual relations: institutional and bureaucratic processes of quality control, dependency reinforced by funding structures, planning, management and evaluation logics and technologies, and a great deal of other means. All these ultimately serve to de-politicise distinctively capitalist ways of thinking, terminologies, norms and practices, re-establishing them as value-neutral, as hegemonic in a field that bears the promise of social and economic change.

In an argument with Margaret Somers (2008) in her call to the civil society to challenge what she calls market fundamentalism, I suggest that the institutionalised civil society of NGOs in all their diversity is not a separate sphere nor can be expected to act as a counter-balance to the market, neither in practice nor on the analytic level. Surely not, as it is subjected to its forces and locked in institutional interrelations which are profoundly unequal and characterised by structural dependency (legal-administrative, financial, etc.) on state and market institutions. Indeed, market fundamentalism is not simply an ideology or a set of policies externally imposed on the civil society; it is rather gradually incorporated into its own logic. Terms like "sustainability" and "efficiency" are adopted and developed by civil society organisations—not only by major international development agencies, but also by many local grassroots initiatives originating in aspiration for social and economic justice, for improvement in women's lives. This is the civil society, as we know it today: it is locked in an institutional entanglement of contradictions and is an active and integral part of it, rather than a coherent separate sphere or a counter-force.

It is precisely the "non-political", claiming to be value-neutral, languages and frameworks of capitalism and neoliberalism—that of rationality, objectivity and seemingly scientific and technical tools like monitoring and evaluation—that make countering these processes so difficult. The capacity of the civil society to politically contradict or balance out neoliberal ideologies is compromised by the subjection of the political to neoliberal contractual engagements. The neoliberal hegemony is also achieved through domination of meaning—which NGOs either unwillingly accept, or uncritically internalise in their own logic and practice. For example, as I have showed, NGOs cannot easily take a stand against the requirement to provide evidence of success. When market logic becomes part of civil society's own common sense, its capacity to challenge market fundamentalism in pursuit of social and economic justice is compromised.

Finally, the expectation that civil society will promote an agenda of social and economic justice (echoed by Somers and representative of a great many academic and activist voices) should grapple with the fact that the vast majority of women's economic empowerment organisations operate in the framework of neoclassical economics, as Chap. 4 further elaborates. By pointing out the complicity of civil society in reproducing the neoliberal hegemony, I do not intend to disqualify its potential to catalyse social and economic change. Civil society interventions constantly do change the ideas, policies and practices collectively understood as neoliberalism—for example, they have been successful in pointing to the structural factors hindering economic independence of migrant and minority women, and there is no doubt that organisations like AEEW and ISI e.V. are making a welcomed and valuable impact on the lives of many women. At the same time, NGOs are also influenced by their engagement with other civil society, state and market actors, and the ideological and material worlds that these actors bring into play. As this chapter has sought to show, these influences evolve in the asymmetrical institutional power structures of the field, where civil society organisations depend on state and increasingly on market actors for their existence and material survival. The move of women's economic rights advocates from resisting neoliberal state policies to contractual engagement in its present form, is not unique to this field, but is indicative to the larger move of civil society—a move from the model of resisting coercion of the state or the market to that of consent and complicity with the state and market institutions. What I find to be the most important contribution of this analysis is that the institutional mechanisms enabling and facilitating this move, and hindering all others, are an ongoing process; and, as such, it reminds us that compliance with neoliberalism is not an ahistorical or irreversible destiny.

References

Bakewell, O., & Garbutt, A. (2005). *The Use and Abuse of the Logical Framework Approach: A Review of International Development NGOs' Experiences*. Swedish International Development Cooperation Agency.

Batliwala, S., & Pittman, A. (2010). *Capturing Change in Women's Realities: A Critical Overview of Current Monitoring & Evaluation Frameworks and Approaches*. Association of Women's Rights in Development (AWID). https://www.awid.org/publications/capturing-change-womens-realities

Berkovitch, N., & Kemp, A. (2010). Economic empowerment of women as a global project: Economic rights in the neo-liberal era. In *Confronting Global Gender Justice* (pp. 176–197). Routledge.

Bloemraad, I., Korteweg, A., & Yurdakul, G. (2008). Citizenship and Immigration: Multiculturalism, Assimilation, and Challenges to the Nation-State. *Annual Review of Sociology, 34*, 153–179.

Bührmann, A. D., & Pongratz, H. J. (2010). Prekäres Unternehmertum. Einführung in ein vernachlässigtes Forschungsfeld. In A. Bührmann & H. J. Pongratz (Eds.), *Prekäres Unternehmertum* (pp. 7–25). VS Verlag für Sozialwissenschaften.

Cornwall, A. (2014). *Women's Empowerment: What Works and Why?* WIDER Working Paper 2014/104. WIDER: World Institute for Development Economics Research, United Nations University.

Cruikshank, B. (1999). *The Will to Empower: Democratic Citizens and Other Subjects*. Cornell University Press.

Dahan-Kalev, H. (2001, November). Tensions in Israeli Feminism: The Mizrahi Ashkenazi Rift. In *Women's Studies International Forum* (Vol. 24, No. 6, pp. 669–684). Pergamon.

Davies, W. (2016). *The Limits of Neoliberalism: Authority, Sovereignty and the Logic of Competition*. Sage.

Duggan, L. (2012). *The Twilight of Equality?: Neoliberalism, Cultural Politics, and the Attack on Democracy*. Beacon Press.

Edwards, M. (2008). *Just Another Emperor?: The Myths and Realities of Philanthrocapitalism*. Demos.

Garbutt, A. (2013). *Monitoring and Evaluation: A Guide for Small and Diaspora NGOs*. International NGO Training and Research Centre (INTRAC). https://www.intrac.org/wpcms/wp-content/uploads/2013/10/ME_A-Guide-for-Small-and-Diaspora-Organisations.pdf

Greenhouse, C. J. (Ed.). (2010). *Ethnographies of Neoliberalism* (p. 1). University of Pennsylvania Press.

Howson, R., & Smith, K. (Eds.). (2008). *Hegemony: Studies in consensus and coercion* (Vol. 56). Routledge.

Kandlik Eltanani, M. (2011). *Inside Me I Combine These Two Themes: Between the Social and the Economic – Trainers in Women's Economic Empowerment Organisations.* M.A. Thesis [unpublished].

Kenny, K., & Scriver, S. (2012). Dangerously Empty? Hegemony and the Construction of the Irish Entrepreneur. *Organization, 19*(5), 615–633.

Lavie, S. (2014). *Wrapped in the Flag of Israel: Mizrahi Single Mothers and Bureaucratic Torture.* University of Nebraska Press.

Pateman, C. (2014). *Sexual Contract.* John Wiley & Sons.

Plehwe, D., Walpen, B. J., & Neunhöffer, G. (2006). *Neoliberal Hegemony: A Global Critique.* Routledge.

Raco, M. (2013). The New Contractualism, the Privatization of the Welfare State, and the Barriers to Open Source Planning. *Planning Practice & Research, 28*(1), 45–64.

Shalhoub-Kevorkian, N. (2014). Palestinian Feminist Critique and the Physics of Power: Feminists Between Thought and Practice. *feminists@ law, 4*(1).

Somers, M. R. (2008). *Genealogies of Citizenship: Markets, Statelessness, and the Right to Have Rights* (Vol. 35). Cambridge University Press.

Ülker, R. B. (2012). *Taking Care of Oneself and Others: 'Ethnic Entrepreneurs' in Berlin.* PhD Dissertation, Central European University.

Weiner, E., & MacRae, H. (2014). The Persistent Invisibility of Gender in EU Policy: Introduction. In E. Weiner & H. MacRae (Eds.), *The Persistent Invisibility of Gender in EU Policy, European Integration online Papers (EIoP), Special,* (1).

CHAPTER 4

Radical Feminists, Mainstream Economics

Interestingly, the field of women's economic empowerment has developed in nearly complete detachment from feminist economics. While women's economic empowerment organisations and practitioners are aware and critical of society and its gendered, racial and class-based inequalities, they are largely acceptant of neoclassical economics, the theory underlying the dominant economic model. In brief, neoclassical economics assumes that markets must be free of substantial government regulation, that human beings make rational choices to maximise utility and profit, that production, consumption and valuation of goods and services are driven by supply and demand. These and other assumptions inform market prices, interest rates, and a great range of mathematical models dominating economics. Women's economic empowerment organisations, particularly with feminist origins, may challenge the patriarchal notion of the male breadwinner; recognise the social importance and burden of women's reproductive labour and care labour; act to strengthen women's voice in their communities. Yet, when it comes to finance, fundamental concepts like value and profit, interest and competition, remain intact and largely unquestioned by virtually all institutional actors involved, albeit they have been critically interrogated for decades by feminist economists.

In fact, interviewees across NGOs were surprised by my question on their approach to economy and economics. One practitioner confirmed that she has never considered it before: "Look, it is the first time I think about it, but all this training for entrepreneurship, I cannot say that this is

I. Michaeli, *Women's Economic Empowerment*,
https://doi.org/10.1007/978-3-030-89281-4_4

exactly a socialist ideology, it is knowing how to play the game, and to know the rules in order to succeed." It is clear that for grassroots women's empowerment organisations, entrepreneurship training and microfinance initiatives are a response to the urgent needs of material survival of their constituencies. In a sense, they have to be pragmatic. Yet, feminists have been engaging pragmatically in many spheres of life, from gender-based violence to reproductive rights, providing direct services and immediate life-saving support without losing radical critique of patriarchy, gender relations and power imbalance, and reproductive and sexual politics. Why, then, couldn't economic empowerment organisations provide the direct support necessary for women to survive in this economy, while holding onto feminist critique of its theoretical foundations?

The science of economics governing social and economic life is an exceptionally authoritative and exclusionary power-knowledge regime. The famous "it's the economy, stupid" line from a US presidential elections campaign is a good illustration of this authoritative power, along with the presumed common sense of inaccessible expert knowledge, and the patronising and belittling approach towards the public. Economics and finance are constructed as inaccessible to the layperson, and even more so to the laywoman. The authority to speak belongs primarily to economics, politicians, business magnates and philanthro-capitalists, or at the very least individuals of certain education and social capital. While the authority to speak is delivered to some, others are fixed in a position of incompetence to discuss and contest financial and economic matters, or even to comprehend them properly. It is thus unsurprising that women's rights organisations were reluctant to engage with the economy and the world of finance. Yet, feminists had little choice but to overcome their reluctance and engage with the feminisation of poverty, the devastating consequences of neoliberal macroeconomic policies for women, and last but not least, the intersectional feminist demand to address realities of less privileged women.

The discourse and practice of women's economic empowerment NGOs, surely in the areas of micro-entrepreneurship and microfinance, leave little doubt as for challenging of neoclassical economics. NGOs and practitioners hold a heterogeneity of positions in relation to concepts and buzzwords as the free market, competition, capitalism, neoliberalism and so on, but not a unified, comprehensive and principled position on the economy in general. There are occasional critical notions on specific neo-liberal policies or anti-social government course of action, such as privatisation of state services or welfare cutbacks. However, there is no comprehensive critical approach or even discussion of economy as such. And, if regarding neoliberal ideas one can still find some difference of perspectives, the neoclassical economics at the core of the dominant economic model goes entirely unquestioned. Neoliberal assumptions about people and societies can be somewhat challenged, but neoclassical economic concepts like value, profit, interest and so on remain intact and unquestioned by virtually all institutional actors involved. Even when there is a general sense of scepticism and mistrust towards the economic and financial sphere and its actors, it does not translate to a comprehensive analysis and coherent approach. That practitioners of women's economic empowerment in all the organisations I encountered do not share a critical analysis of the economy or of economics as a field of knowledge, serves to demonstrate how ingrained capitalism and neoclassical economics are, as a form of common sense. In neo-Gramscian terms, I found that all the actors in the field are complicit in reproducing the hegemony of neoclassical economics as a discourse, a regime of truth. In this context, an alternative economy does not exist as a point of reference or even fantasy—it is simply put beyond imagination.

Critical scholars underscore that neoliberalism is imagined as the only social and economic order possible, and capitalism is imagined as the only possible economic system. The scientific base of mainstream economics and the finance sector is taken for granted and rarely questioned, if at all (Hall et al., 2013). Even the global financial crisis of late 2000s which has shaken entire national economies, did not lead to extensive questioning of dominant economic theories and of the idealised entrepreneurial risk-taking subject (Tedmanson et al., 2012). While economic transactions in everyday life are multiple and do deviate from capitalist logics and forms, they are far from discursive recognition by mainstream and critical scholars alike (Gibson-Graham, 1997).

Feminist economics, albeit nearly non-existent in the sphere of economic empowerment, is a thriving field of knowledge, which has solidified around 1980s and 1990s. It is a heterogeneous and rather inter-disciplinary field, ranging from applying gender lens to neoclassical economics, to questioning its foundations altogether and exploring non-capitalist economic models. However, while feminist scholarship has had a transformative effect on many disciplines, the field of economics is rather the exception, where neoclassical economics maintained its iron stronghold despite extensive feminist critique (Benería et al., 2003). The contributions of feminist economists have been far more successful in leaving an imprint on other social sciences. The valuation of reproductive labour, the importance of care work in sustaining human life, and even the redefinition of what economy is, in social and relational (rather than profit-maximisation) terms, are among the main contributions.

It is impossible to say that these ideas do not inform the field of women's economic empowerment. Indeed, they have made their way to inform and shape many feminist discourses and movements around the world. Yet, in women's economic empowerment discourses and practices these ideas are delineated by the social/economic binary, and relegated to the social realm. Society is the realm where critical perspectives on society and injustice reside, where gendered and racial and class-based inequalities may be interrogated and addressed. Economy, on the other hand, is often reduced to neoclassical economics and the world of finance, which is constructed as a scientific, objective and value-neutral object of knowledge. This implicit set of binaries—by which society is subjective, dynamic and fluid, while economy is objective, permanent and fixed—certainly corresponds with the gender binary.

Beyond women's economic empowerment, and even on its margins, feminist and other critical scholars, practitioners and activists do question the economy and its neoliberal course In response to this repeated questioning of neoliberal macroeconomic policies and their devastating effects on women, international financial and political institutions, such as the World Bank and the European Union, invest extensive resources to assert compatibility between the gender equality agenda and the dominant economic model. This compatibility is not always self-evident. As previously noted, the World Bank has gone to great lengths to establish a correlation between gender equality and economic growth, a foundational aspect of capitalism. Research institutions affiliated with the World Bank and the European Union, among other powerful institutions, produce an immense body of research informing scientific, policy, and public discourses, research whose theoretical and ideological foundations are in fact aligned with neoliberal macroeconomic policies (Prügl, 2017, Elomäki, 2015). With extensive knowledge production machinery serving to legitimise the dominant economic mode from a gender equality perspective, scrutinising its theoretical core, the neoclassical economics, is unsurprisingly out of reach for most practitioners of women's economic empowerment.

The discourse on investment in women as "smart economics" has further enhanced the appeal of neoclassical economics for many women's rights advocates and economic empowerment practitioners. This so-called business case for gender equality has made its way to international and national policy tables and advocacy corridors worldwide. The business case is the argument that gender equality and advancement of women is profitable: Hence, advancement of women in social, economic and political life is good for the national economy; inclusion of women in management and directorates of companies is good for their business performance, and so on. It is easy for a feminist critical of neoliberalism to reject this discourse on theoretical and political grounds, as it subjects our rights to market terms and interests. Yet, imagine a women's rights advocate who has been ignored by policy makers for decades, and is suddenly listened to, the moment she mentions the business case. Such "win-win" narratives dominate much of women's economic empowerment field, in the spirit of neoliberal contract examined in detail in Chap. 3.

The most pronounced engagement of women's economic empowerment organisations with mainstream economics is around women's access to finance. The framing of access to finance as the problem enables microfinance as the solution. There is no doubt that access to finance truly is more difficult for women. The importance of access to finance has been reiterated in research and policy documents, and subsequently incorporated in the development of various projects and policy solutions, nationally and globally. However, framing access to finance as the root cause of women's economic disadvantage normalises and legitimises the dominant economic model. In the neoliberal paradigm, this makes sense. Yet, from a feminist Marxist position for example, the root cause is not access to finance, but the unequal distribution of wealth (Federici, 2014). Unequal distribution of wealth persists on global scale between North and South, and on national levels among racialised, ethnic and national groups, and it is always gendered. Yet, when the market economy is taken for granted, questions of distributive justice become obscure, and the main path to empowerment becomes access to finance.

In Chap. 2, we have seen that microfinance has played an important role in the de-politicisation and financialisation of women's economic empowerment, its neoliberal turn from collective to the individual, and from a broad social justice agenda to isolated economic objectives of individual income generation. Critical accounts of microfinance schemes indeed point to their double function: their focus on the individual at the expense of collective action, and their detachment from broader social change agendas, thereby serving functions of containing, disciplining and de-politicising the poor and the communities historically oppressed. This is achieved, first, by interpreting poverty as a given, a situation in which various individuals find themselves, rather than societal or political problem. Poverty, however, is created; it is not a natural given condition, nor an accidental by-product of an economic system. Economic systems of complex and differentiated accumulation and distribution of resources generate wealth for some as much as they generate its absence for others. Historical and contemporary processes, from colonialism to structural adjustments and climate disasters, shape economic inequalities of today. By targeting the individual, microfinance places the responsibility on the shoulders of the poor, while dismissing the historical and current structural factors that create and sustain poverty. To call on a biblical metaphor beloved by the neoliberal spirit of development, microfinance bears the promise of teaching poor people how to fish, while obscuring the fact that the pond might be empty, the water might be poisoned, and the fish might be long dead.

It is important to note that microfinance in itself is not a single unified paradigm. While the harsh critique is well deserved by the top-down microfinance industry as such, grassroots economic empowerment organisations driven by genuine commitment to respond to people's needs deserve a more nuanced look. Some of their microfinance programmes differ not only in their impact and results, but also in their ideological underpinnings, in the broader agendas they constitute, and in the socio-political and economic contexts where they take place. As Caroline Shenaz Hossein (2016) shows in her ethnographic research on micro-lending in Jamaica, Guyana, and Haiti, while in some contexts, socio-economic and racial inequalities are reproduced through microfinance, in others they are more successfully challenged. Bottom-up approach, collective systems (credit unions), rootedness in people's histories are some of the factors that make a difference.

A classification offered by Linda Mayoux (2006) distinguishes between three paradigms of microfinance. The feminist empowerment paradigm views microfinance as a tool for the economic, social and political empowerment of women, is motivated by gender equality and human rights, and relies (historically, at least) on socialist feminist critiques of capitalism. The poverty alleviation paradigm employs microfinance for poverty reduction, and is likely to target women because of their traditional household roles or higher levels of poverty. Finally, the financial self-sustainability paradigm is likely to target women because of their higher repayment rates and the contribution of their economic activity to economic growth, and is motivated by neoliberal agendas and ideologies of self-reliance. Grassroots projects and organisations rarely embody a pure model or discourse, and we have already traced some of their enmeshments and shifts over time—shifts that were driven by transformations in the external context and in the life cycles of the institution itself, its change of people and of activity. I came across organisations that were evidently founded by feminists critical of capitalism, where the current staff members strongly shared the commitment to gender equality and the empowerment of women, but have not questioned neoliberal ideologies and agendas. What such classification allows is to identify the competing logics in the field and to observe the dominance of some over others in given projects and organisations.

The critique of microfinance as a global strategy to alleviate poverty and overcome economic marginalisation exceeds the field of women's economic empowerment. Although earlier development of micro-entrepreneurship model took place in global South countries since the 1950s and again later, since 1970s, undertaken by women's rights organisations as a means of supporting women's economic survival and independence, microfinance truly rose to prominence through the well-known work of Muhammad Yunus in Bangladesh. Yunus founded the Grameen Bank and provided microcredit to entrepreneurs too poor to receive regular bank loans. The reported record of success in terms of loan repayment brought him and his model international recognition. Microcredit was then enthusiastically embraced by local and international development and aid organisations. In 2006, Yunus and the Grameen Bank were awarded the Nobel Peace Prize for their contribution to the alleviation of poverty as an essential component of global peacebuilding. Since then, the microfinance model has been exported not only throughout the global South, but also to the global North, - and branches of the Grameen Bank have opened in a number of cities in the United States, for example.

Microfinance continues to be celebrated globally, even as overwhelming evidence points to its failure, as a whole, to benefit poor. Why? One reason is the extensive knowledge production machinery operated by INGOs and microfinance institutions that reinforces the narrative of its success and manufactures the evidence to support it, filtering the more critical accounts by scholars actually grounded in local contexts (Karim, 2011). I find the most convincing explanation on the persistence of microfinance in its temptation as a win-win strategy (Hickel, 2015). For activists and grassroots groups, it is one of the few means available to respond to the material needs of marginalised communities, with good chances of securing public or private funding even in the most neoliberal of governments. For institutions and individuals in power, it bears the promise of eradicating poverty without transforming economic and geopolitical power relations or their racial, ethnic and gender order, and is therefore not threatening. This promise allows microfinance to survive many empirical records of failure and to maintain its reputation as success. Not only can the economic and political elites address poverty without losing their power and privilege—they can even get a return on their investment and profit from it. Increasingly, microfinance institutions sign business agreements with multinational corporations and enhance expansion of markets into the global South, facilitating access to new consumers and enriching North-based corporations (Karim, 2011). Digital microfinance, although beyond the scope of this research, provides us a glimpse in the privatised version of microfinance and its win-win appeal. Platforms as the San Francisco–based Kiva.org allow individuals to lend amounts starting from $25 USD to borrowers worldwide, to "make a big change in someone's life", as the website reads. In this person-to-person microfinance, benevolent individuals in wealthy countries consume highly emotional narratives about the life-changing effects their $25 USD are going to mean for individuals in low- and middle-income countries. Not only do these narratives contrast with the actual accounts of the borrowers, they also reinforce neo-colonial gendered and racialised relations characteristic of mainstream development discourses, and, importantly, leave the unequal distribution of wealth entirely out of the picture.

Let us look closely at one specific financial aspect central to the field of women's economic empowerment via entrepreneurship and microfinance. Nowhere is the hegemony of neoclassical economics as evident as in the microcredit interest rate. For those new to the world of microfinance, one of the most surprising discoveries is that microfinance loans for marginalised women are often issued at particularly high interest rates. This might seem puzzling, that marginalised women, struggling to find a way out of poverty or economic distress, are offered microcredit loans at interest rates that are similar or higher than those offered to wealthier people by the banks. In fact, in global South countries the rates are often higher than in Israel and Germany, and generally vary greatly. While global averages are at about 35%, in some countries they can go far over 50%. The logic of the microfinance model provides an explanation that is evidently plausible and convincing enough for the majority of its practitioners, from bank clerks to feminist activists. Namely, that a small-size loan is "more expensive" for the bank or the microcredit provider—management of multiple small loans requires more work and costs from the provider; and, furthermore, a marginalised woman also requires additional financial and entrepreneurial education, consulting and training. This logic was contested by only one disillusioned veteran practitioner of an Israeli NGO, who indicated the isolation of her position: "Listen, I don't like this perception, not at all, but I think I am the only one in the field who does not accept the approach of microfinance. [...] ...what they [microcredit providers] say, they are somehow complicit in the story that the banks tell, they say that because the woman is marginalised and disadvantaged, and the bank does not like her and all that, and she requires more investment, then she will pay a higher interest rate. This is the overall approach in the world, by the way also with [Muhammad] Yunes and all that, the interest rates were quite high. They said, for the woman it is actually not so important, as long as she gets the loan, she will not be doing these calculations, whether it is 7% or 9%, she will not sit at home and calculate, so it somehow works for them. I say it is offensive to think like that."

Interest rates as such are in consensus in the field of women's economic empowerment. Although the provision of credit is essential for micro-entrepreneurship to function, most NGOs in the field have very little or no power at all in deciding on the interest rate. This is the case for NGOs providing entrepreneurship training rather than direct credit, but also for microfinance institutions working in partnership with banks and large funding bodies. Interest rates, as most financial aspects of microcredit, are accepted by NGOs as a given. They are not perceived as arenas that can be contested, questioned and change, but as coming from above—from the bank or the financing body, from the objective necessity to cover operation costs, and so on. At times, practitioners in the field do call for lower interest rates, but the justification of their demand is confined to practical considerations and possibilities of the women (e.g., when women face difficulties in repaying), rather than challenging the logic of the model itself on political grounds. These financial matters, the financial content and logic of the field, are constructed to reside beyond the field's politics. Underlying the justifications for higher interest rate is the axiom that microfinance must be profitable, and this logic of profitability has become the common sense of the field (Berkovitch & Kemp, 2010). The globalisation of women's economic empowerment, as noted, has created a discursive field with its own commercialised logics, norms and boundaries. While practitioners do not share a unified and comprehensive critical discourse on the economics and financial logics of microfinance, the sense of injustice, such as the one voiced by the practitioner above, comes across loud and clear. That same practitioner challenged the logic by which a marginalised woman who is "more expensive" to the system than a wealthier client should pay for the difference herself. Instead, she opted for a different kind of logic, one that prioritises the common good and the larger benefit for society in improving women's economic situation. It would be so much better for the state to help her and her family escape the cycle of poverty, she suggested. In this alternative perspective, the investment in women pays off to the state, even if they "cost more" to the bank or the microcredit program—and perhaps the state could bear those excessive costs. The practitioner makes clear that hers is a rather isolated position; the majority of her colleagues accept the financial logic of microfinance, and it is true for economic empowerment field at large.

During a staff meeting at AEEW, I observed that the members did not have a shared position on such critical issues as the entrance of additional microfinancing institutions. In that meeting, AEEW staff members had different opinions on whether the entrance of additional microcredit providers, and the increased competition between them, would be good or bad for marginalised women. Some voiced that market competition in is a good thing, and that competition among institutions is in itself positive for the people. Others rejected this predicament, argued that the competition between microcredit providers would not benefit the women, and might lead to higher, not lower interest rates. Staff members were thus divided in their assessment of the potential entrance of additional microfinancing actors to the field. I found this exchange, which came up spontaneously during a staff meeting, particularly telling in demonstrating the lack of common analysis of the very foundations of the free market and its predicaments.

Practitioners with expertise in microfinance admit that competition among microcredit providers will increase the percentage of interest rates, but point out that it would also increase their quantity, thereby meeting the needs of larger populations. The entrance of financing institutions that are not banks—like insurance companies and pension funds—is seen as a positive and desired development by many practitioners. According to this position, provision of microcredit for marginalised women needs to be made profitable for microfinance institutions and for the banks and commercial institutions funding them. The assumption is that this profit needs to come from the women themselves, so that the lending institutions do not need to raise funds from the state or from philanthropy. While bank loans can be subsidised, making a difference, for example, of 7% interest rate for a bank loan versus 12% for a microcredit loan, many clients either prefer to avoid encounters with banks, or have no other choice, because the bank would not provide them a loan. Examining data from a number of countries in Asia and the global South, Protitch (2007) reaches the conclusion that interest rate ceilings that are too low to cover the costs of the microfinancing institutions (MFIs) lead them to decrease the scope of services and the number of loans they are able to provide, particularly in rural areas: "[T]hus, interest rate ceilings that do not allow MFIs to cover their costs only harm the population".

An accompanying rhetoric to the justification of high interest rates is that for poor people, the mere access to credit is no less valuable symbolically than the actual economic profit they stand to gain from it. The ability to ascribe significant value to personal empowerment, self-confidence and respect from the community could have been a welcomed break from the logic of financial profit above all. However, this symbolic aspect is valued exclusively and excessively in relation to marginalised peoples. Practitioners and policy-makers often voice the idea that a woman's participation in the programme will not necessarily increase her income in a substantial manner, but she will feel better about herself, and her family and community will respect her more. It would be unimaginable to suggest that although the bank will not receive the money back, the director would feel good about helping people in need. Where the profit can be compromised or even dismissed in favour of social values, it is worthwhile considering whose profit is dismissible, and whose profit is not.

I have reiterated that a consensus was established around the need for marginalised women to pay higher interest rates, because they are more "expensive" to the credit system. Underlying this consensus is the axiom that microfinance has to be profitable. Yet, what causes marginalised women to be "more expensive" in the first place, and why is there a consensus around them being the ones paying for this difference? If the factors leading to and fixing these women in poverty are recognised as structural and societal, rooted in gender and racial, ethnic and class hierarchies that are by no means her own fault or responsibility, why should this social injustice be privatised and paid by the women? Why, in other words, should they pay the price of their own discrimination and marginalisation, for being "more expensive"? Cost-effectiveness calculations for microfinance institutions limit the analysis and the discourse of the field to hard numbers of neoclassical economics, wrapped in a neoliberal logic.

The perception that the individual marginalised woman is the one to pay the interest rate—high as it needs to be for the microfinance institution to cover the costs and to survive, for the bank to make profit, for the project to become sustainable—is by and large accepted and taken for granted. Having that said, feminists in the field of economic empowerment understand very well that their constituencies are economically disadvantaged for structural reasons beyond their control, and that the interest to get them out of poverty is a collective one. However, this collective social interest does not translate to interest in the economic or financial sense; the social is lost in neoclassical economic translation.

It is well known that the vast majority of microfinance recipients around the world are women. Women's ideal candidacy for microfinance is rationalised by a range of gender norms and by certain arrangements of the political economy of the family (Cornwall et al., 2008, Berkovitch & Kemp, 2010). Feminist scholars define this representation as an image of the Good Woman: a reliable and obedient recipient of credit, who is capable to generating income yet whose primary commitment lies with her identity as a wife and a mother (Chakravarti, 2008). The Good Woman image entails a paradox within the neoliberal logic: If economic empowerment is intended to make women fit for market economy, that is, to produce subjectivity of a rational economic actor concerned with the maximisation of his profit, how are we to make sense of this representation? How are women to become rational, economic, profit-seeking self-interested entrepreneurial actors, while fitting the image of the committed mother and wife? How is the Good Woman different from homo economicus? These assumptions do not only dominate marketing materials of microfinance institutions; they play a range of disciplinary functions towards the women who are credit recipients. And, as we shall see, this proper behaviour is reinforced even when it goes against or differs from what is perceived to be proper entrepreneurial behaviour.

Microfinance institutions often offer women a friendly environment with an interpersonal contact. Friederike Welter (2004), in her research on the institutional and legal context for female entrepreneurship in Germany, finds a series of gender-specific needs, related to gender-specific challenges that women face on the path to entrepreneurship. These challenges encompass access to finance and potential discrimination from the side of bankers. According to my own findings and earlier research, women micro-entrepreneurs prefer to avoid major financial institutions, experiencing the atmosphere as male dominated, inaccessible, unfriendly.

Microfinance programmes often pride themselves for offering this much-needed interpersonal contact to their constituencies. This personalised approach to economic transactions and loan-management creates an impression of a more humane and empathic economy, in contrast to the alienated, inaccessible and "heartless" major financial institutions. However—and this is my principal argument in this section—there is an ambivalent twist to these interpersonal contacts. As we shall see, the same interpersonal contact also functions as a means of formal and informal social and economic control.

As microfinance institutions offer worse interest rates than the bank, women receiving these loans fall into a few following categories. They have no other choice because either they have been already rejected by the bank or they are not entitled to a bank loan, or as above, they experience banking institutions as inaccessible and value the interpersonal contact and emotional support offered by microfinance programmes designed for women. Women's preference for positive interpersonal contact came strongly both in the German and the Israeli interviews. Across countries it is recognised that women can relate better to female loan officers (Cheston & Kuhn, 2002). German and Israeli microcredit agencies servicing women indeed emphasised the importance of the interpersonal contact they offer women. This is in fact their major advantage, in addition to being able to offer a loan to women who would otherwise be refused by the bank. This interpersonal contact is generally an employee of the microcredit programme. It is likely to be a woman, possibly from the same racialised, ethnic or national community of the clients' target group. Her function in the organisation depends on the organisational structure. In smaller microcredit organisation, like the German NGO Goldrausch e.V., it is part of the Coordinator's tasks, as she is the sole paid staff member of the organisation. In a larger organisation, such as The Koret Israel Economic Development Funds (KIEDF), these are Field Consultants, and this is the main component of their work. However, across organisational differences, both large and small microfinance programmes have emphasised the value this interpersonal dimension holds for women.

How then does the interpersonal contact serve as a means of formal and informal social and economic control? Let us take KIEDF as an example. Its credit-granting process in KIEDF consists of the following stages, with the women applying and receiving loans. The first stage is a phone interview with the Coordination, a provision of a recent bank statement and balance sheets. Then, a preliminary decision is made by the Fund and forwarded to the Field Consultant. The Field Consultant meets the client in her business, which is most often her home, to prepare the application form. The form is then submitted to the Fund, and, upon approval, filed to the bank with recommendation. The Coordinator of KIEDF's microfinance programme that serves mostly Palestinian women with Israeli citizenship emphasised that while her own opinion is important, the opinion of the FC "can even be more important, more realistic". The FC's impressions from visiting the business and the assessment of its potential, of the client's personality and capacities, may change the initial picture. The FC does not only hold power to influence the approval or rejection of the grant request, she is also responsible to maintain contact with the client, to consult and advise her. No less crucial is her function when the client has difficulties to meet return payments. "Unlike the bank, there is this accompaniment of the consultant, someone who comes and gives the tips that can actually get the whole business going [...] the accompaniment is very important. And then in the advanced stages, if the client is behind on her payments, the FC checks on her. When there is the FC, women feel ashamed [when not making payments to return the loan] and they want to do the maximum in order to pay."

Shame is thus triggered in women in the context of feminist rhetoric and practice of interpersonal contact which de facto serves as a means of social and economic control over these women. Formal control resembles the bank: it is the phone call when the payment is not made. Informal means of control are more specific to microfinance programmes, as they rely on the interpersonal dimension and trigger the mechanism of shame in distinct ways. Although this is also true for banks, and speaks to the increased tendency of women to repay loans, the closer interpersonal contact and the emotional bond and a sense of commitment established, especially with a woman from the same community, evidently makes shame a more powerful mechanism of social and economic control. Having observed that, I began noticing shame coming up quite frequently in accounts and research about microfinance. While in this case shame operates through interpersonal contact with a representative of the microfinance programme, in other microfinance programmes it operates through loan groups, where women are each other's guarantee, and through other community structures mobilised in the service of peer pressure to repay.

Drawing on the work of Sandra Lee Bartky (1997), I understand shame as more than a feeling or emotion—rather, as a barometer for society, as a mode of disclosure about what is socially constructed as shameful, and who is the subject expected to bear shame. The financial chain of microfinance involves banks, state authorities, philanthropists, development funds, microcredit programmes and marginalised women. In this chain, the shame is being located exclusively and fully in the latter segment, on the women. In other words, when women are unable to repay the loan, they are expected to be ashamed—not state authorities, not the microfinance providers, and not the banks. Meanwhile, the same setting created to cater to women's needs for a friendly interpersonal contact is leveraged to instil shame and pressure them into repayments at any cost. A set of sociocultural normative and ethical assumptions informs the social contract established between women and microfinance programmes, and, by extension, the other institutional actors involved. In this contract, what emerges is the unquestionable social and cultural importance placed on the payback of loans as an absolute ethical value, which fully justifies the triggering of shame. However, this value is far from being absolute, on the contrary. The market is characterised by ongoing bailouts and erasures of multi-million debts, bailouts that more often than not are rather shameless, for corporations and individual billionaires alike. Although human beings are prone to shame, as such, shame is not self-evident in market economy. Banks are not ashamed to take people's homes and corporations are not ashamed to displace millions of people, to cause environmental damage or to fire people for the sake of profit. Individuals embodying these institutions are rarely expected to be personally ashamed. Microfinance institutions lending money to poor people at extremely high rates are not expected to feel shame when these people fail to pay back, nor when they go into considerable lengths and sacrifice just to pay the loan back. Shame comes about across national and regional contexts as a significant function and mechanism of microfinancing, either implicit or explicit, and underlies some of the 'smart economics' discourses.

In addition to being a profoundly heteronormative means of disciplining women, the Good Woman discourses also produce problematic images of men who are too irresponsible to meet repayment demands, and who, as husbands, are either "abusive or useless" and cannot be expected to invest their profits into family welfare (Chakravarti, 2008). This could be heard clearly in the words of practitioners in Israel and Germany, respectively: "every time we tried to work with men, it turned out to be a disaster", and, "when a man comes, he doesn't even have a proper business plan, he immediately wants his office, his fancy car… women are more careful in preparing detailed business plans, examining every budget line for necessity".

While women's perceived tendency to take less risks turns them into better candidates for microcredit, it has been proven to work against them in major financing institutions. Not rushing to rent an office may make a good impression on the microcredit consultant, indicating a responsible and careful entrepreneurial attitude. For example, a staff member of microfy, an Israeli organisation working with refugees, was critical of male clients, refugees and asylum seekers, who tended to sign rental contracts they had no means to afford. This practice served as an evidence of irrational and irresponsible business practice. Yet, referring back to Welter's work (2004), businesses operating from home, rather than a rented office, are considered by banking institutions to be less professional, and are less likely to receive financing. Women from marginalised backgrounds, migrant and refugee entrepreneurs, seem to find themselves between a rock and a hard place: playing it too safe or taking unreasonable risks, being over-ambitious or appearing not professional enough.

Women are not passive recipients of empowerment and entrepreneurship training. The field of women's economic empowerment and microcredit operates on a set of normative assumptions about women, their needs and their conduct. These gendered assumptions enable to design programmes and practices to respond to women's needs; yet, as we can see, these practices also serve as means of control within the power relationship established among civil society organisations and their constituencies. Cruickshank notes that "technologies of citizenship secure voluntary compliance of citizens and promote their autonomy and capacity to act upon their self-interests, but they also shape and enlist these interests and wills" (1999: 4). These interests and wills, however, are shaped by multiple and at times conflicting discourses, at times leaving practitioners frustrated when a woman exercises agency and expresses needs and wills at odds with entrepreneurial ideals. A business consultant from the Tel Aviv University Clinic talked with astonishment and almost envy of women from a marginalised background—Palestinian women in Jaffa, who nonetheless bring forth quite a few conditions to their desired employment. According to the business consultant's account, this has to do with the fact that many of them need money only as a second salary, or simply wish to do something outside home. "They want comfortable hours, to do something they know, with a salary sheet, without registering. No supermarket and no cleaning. No IRS stuff". The business consultant proclaimed that she herself would also like to spend more time with her child or to have comfortable hours, but this is not an option for her. With irony and self-awareness she commented that "every deviation of a woman from the neoliberal mode is very challenging. They do not think in business or capitalist patterns". In these interactions, women clearly refuse the image of the driven entrepreneur, one who is ready to sacrifice everything for success. Instead, they negotiate entrepreneurship as an activity and as a subject position. They are willing to do it on their own terms, and they are not willing to give up on their time with the family and to turn their lives around completely.

The reluctance towards critical engagement with economic and financial logic is evident not only in the practice of civil society organisations in the field of women's economic empowerment and micro-entrepreneurship, but also in the critical and feminist research of the field. Even when engaging from a perspective attentive to neoliberal ideologies, discourses, and practices in the field, feminist research often overlooks its financial raison d'être: The concrete material information, the range of loans, the rates of interest, the conditions of repayment, are all often ignored. These findings led me to a partly argumentative dialogue with Helene Ahl and Susan Marlow, who point to feminist post-structuralist analysis of gender as a solution to the current epistemological limitations of entrepreneurship and gender research. The authors claim that entrepreneurship is "embedded within the prevailing gendered order which privileges masculinity as the dominant mode of thought, deed and action" (2012: 556). While I agree with this assessment, I suggest that the situation is far more complicated. Entrepreneurship, as a field of practice and research, is embedded not just within the prevailing gendered order, but also within the prevailing economic order of capitalism and neoclassical economics. The authors question the gendered nature of entrepreneurship, but its economic theoretical underpinnings remain transparent in their discussion. What is missing for Ahl and Marlow, and what in my opinion cannot be overlooked, is the economy itself. Furthermore, gender dynamics of entrepreneurship are embedded in local and global power structures that position different groups of women in radically different positions of access, power and privilege. The capacity of certain groups of women to free themselves from domestic labour, for example, is directly enabled by the gendered division of labour on both local and global levels.

Scholarly engagement with entrepreneurship may depart from the normative gender order, but participants and practitioners of economic empowerment and entrepreneurship training cannot walk away that easily.

Because grassroots organisations aim to respond in sensitive ways to the realities of women's lives in patriarchal societies, on the one hand, and on the other hand, inevitably respond to the realities of the market economy, they appear to be locked in a dissonance. The gendered division of labour in traditional communities certainly limits women's entrepreneurial potential, but deviating from this order, as Ahl and Marlow appear to suggest, also means deviating from women's lives. And so, grassroots organisations work within the constraints of both the existing gendered order and the existing economic order, challenging them where they find possible, and expressing frustration when participants insist on remaining within their social world, and hold on their traditional gender roles. Thus, I suggest that the post-structuralist approach, as offered by Ahl and Mahlow for critical gender and entrepreneurship research, must remain attentive not only to the epistemological limitations of the field, but also to its structural and material conditions. Otherwise, the risk is to underestimate the institutional, structural obstacles that complicate economic survival for marginalised women, and to underestimate the external factors that lead women's grassroots organisations to turn to economic empowerment and entrepreneurship training in the first place, despite the significant problems and paradoxes it involves.

References

Ahl, H., & Marlow, S. (2012). Exploring the Dynamics of Gender, Feminism and Entrepreneurship: Advancing Debate to Escape a Dead End? *Organization, 19*(5), 543–562.

Bartky, S. L. (1997). *Foucault, Femininity, and the Modernization of Patriarchal Power*. Routledge.

Benería, L., Berik, G., & Floro, M. S. (2003). *Gender, Development, and Globalization: Economics as if All People Mattered*. Routledge.

Berkovitch, N., & Kemp, A. (2010). Economic Empowerment of Women as a Global Project: Economic Rights in the Neo-Liberal Era. In *Confronting Global Gender Justice* (pp. 176–197). Routledge.

Chakravarti, U. (2008). Beyond the Mantra of Empowerment: Time to Return to Poverty, Violence and Struggle. *IDS Bulletin, 39*(6), 10–17. Institute of Development Studies. http://bulletin.ids.ac.uk/idsbo/article/view/711

Cheston, S., & Kuhn, L. (2002). Empowering Women Through Microfinance. *Draft, Opportunity International, 64*, 1–64.

Cornwall, A., Gideon, J., & Wilson, K. (2008). Introduction: Reclaiming Feminism: Gender and Neoliberalism. *IDS Bulletin, 39*(6), 1–9.

Cruikshank, B. (1999). *The Will to Empower: Democratic Citizens and Other Subjects*. Cornell University Press.

Elomäki, A. (2015). The Economic Case for Gender Equality in the European Union: Selling Gender Equality to Decision-Makers and Neoliberalism to Women's Organizations. *European Journal of Women's Studies, 22*(3), 288–302.

Federici, S. (2014). From Commoning to Debt: Financialization, Microcredit, and the Changing Architecture of Capital Accumulation. *South Atlantic Quarterly, 113*(2), 231–244.

Gibson-Graham, J. K. (1997). The End of Capitalism (As We Knew It): A Feminist Critique of Political Economy. *Capital & Class, 21*(2), 186–188.

Hall, S., Massey, D., & Rustin, M. (2013). After Neoliberalism: Analysing the Present. *Soundings, 53*(53), 8–22.

Hickel, J. (2015, June 10). The Microfinance Delusion: Who Really Wins? *The Guardian*. https://www.theguardian.com/global-development-professionals-network/2015/jun/10/the-microfinance-delusion-who-really-wins

Hossein, C. S. (2016). *Politicized Microfinance: Money, Power, and Violence in the Black Americas*. University of Toronto Press.

Karim, L. (2011). *Microfinance and Its Discontents: Women in Debt in Bangladesh*. University of Minnesota Press.

Mayoux, L. (2006). Women's Empowerment Through Sustainable Microfinance: Rethinking "Best Practice". *Eldis Gender Guide*, 47–62.

Protitch, M. (2007, May). The Role of Interest Rates in Microfinance: Why They Are So High and How They Affect Consumer Behaviour. In *Seminar Papers in Development Economics*. Berlin: Humboldt University.

Prügl, E. (2017). Neoliberalism with a Feminist Face: Crafting a New Hegemony at the World Ban k. *Feminist Economics, 23*(1), 30–53.

Tedmanson, D., Verduyn, K., Essers, C., & Gartner, W. B. (2012). Critical Perspectives in Entrepreneurship Research. *Organization, 19*(5), 531–541.

Welter, F. (2004). The Environment for Female Entrepreneurship in Germany. *Journal of Small Business and Enterprise Development*. https://doi.org/10.1108/14626000410537155

CHAPTER 5

Construction of the Entrepreneurial Self

While analysing the macro level of institutional power relations locates the project of economic empowerment of women in its sociopolitical context, the actual project of empowering and training women to become entrepreneurs remains to be understood. In the previous chapters, we have seen the tensions that arise in the convergence of different and often oppositional ideologies, values and priorities in the field of women's economic empowerment. Institutional power relations operate to effectively depoliticise and mitigate these multiple tensions, employing distinctively neoliberal mechanisms, such as market-based evaluation techniques. These institutional power relations constitute a complex interplay of coercion and consent, by which civil society organisations become active participants in the re-production of the hegemonic order, as indeed the hegemony of neoclassical economics and astonishingly high interest rates in microfinance.

In November 2012, the Van Leer Institute in Jerusalem hosted the conference "Changing Capitalism, Changing Feminism: Women's Social and Economic Citizenship in the Age of Neoliberalism". Ayelet Ilani, co-founder of the Association for Economic Empowerment for Women and its first director, shared the following experience in her lecture: "When we started working in the field of service provision, [entrepreneurship] trainings and [microcredit] loans, we had no idea what we are getting ourselves into, how hard it is, how binding, and how much the change that we wish for – to bring women out of poverty – is oppositional to, and in

I. Michaeli, *Women's Economic Empowerment*,
https://doi.org/10.1007/978-3-030-89281-4_5

dissonance with, the entire economic, political and cultural environment in which we live."

The notions of dissonance and paradox in this powerful statement underlie much of the discourse and everyday practice of women's economic empowerment. Paradox emerges as an inseparable and integral defining feature of the field. It is not limited to the level of the desired change, that is, to bring women out of poverty under the factual conditions of growing socio-economic gaps. On its face, the chosen strategy for economic empowerment of women—entrepreneurship—is paradoxical in itself. Entrepreneurship is not traditionally associated with women, even less so with low-income and migrant women. The classical image of the risk-taking entrepreneur assumes venture capital and a range of resources that are not self-evident for marginalised populations. Women's economic empowerment organisations recognise these gaps, and so the entrepreneurship training that they offer often combines formal business and financial training, assistance in access to credit, and a process of personal empowerment, involving a range of tools designed to transform behaviour, perception and consciousness of the participant. This intervention is locked in a paradox between the structural and the individual: On the one hand, women's economic empowerment organisations understand perfectly well that the underprivileged socio-economic reality of their constituencies is a result of external social and economic forces. On the other hand, as we shall see, there is an extensive the replication of highly individualised notions like "entrepreneurial spirit", "personal spark", "that attitude!" that are so characteristic of hegemonic entrepreneurial discourses. This tension between the structural problem and the individualised nature of attempted remedies flows throughout the macro and micro levels of the field.

Constituencies of women's economic empowerment encompass a diversity of national, racialised and ethnic groups with fundamentally different histories and realities of citizenship. In Germany, immigrant women entrepreneurs come primarily from Turkey, Poland, Italy, Greece and Russia, although in ISI e.V. there is significant representation of women from other countries too, particularly from the regions of Latin America and Asia. In Israel, this is an indigenous group of Arab-Palestinian women, including Bedouin women, and the different ethnic groups of Jewish women: Mizrahi women and women immigrants from the Former Soviet Union and Ethiopia defined as olim (repatriates) by the Law of Return that grants citizenship to Jews and their descendants. What brings these women together as participants of economic empowerment programmes is their economic distress, marginalisation in the labour market, and lack of decent employment opportunities. However, the reasons for this distress, its history and the mechanisms perpetuating it might be different—indeed, are fundamentally different—among the groups. The intersection of gender, racial and class-based oppression is a common experience for the women who come to these programmes, yet these intersections are rooted in different albeit interlinked historical and political trajectories. Differences of education and social class, economic capital, marital status, migration generation and so on are all crucial factors in shaping one's economic status and citizenship, reminding us of the irreducible heterogeneity of each racialised, ethnic and national group. The incorporation of certain members of marginalised groups into the elite and privileged parts by the neoliberal order is not to be ignored, albeit beyond the scope here. In the Israeli context, Palestinian women and Mizrahi women have different histories and are on the opposite sides of the colonial regime, even as they meet in the same economic empowerment organisations. In the German context, the challenges Italian women with EU citizenship might experience are not identical to those of Turkish women, or migrants from Latin America, even as they all meet in the same women's entrepreneurship course. The dynamics of economic citizenship and its ethno-national and racial dimensions will be analysed in detail and discussed in Chap. 6. Here, I proceed to focus on the micro level, that is, on the discourses and practices of economic empowerment and on the subject they envision, the empowered woman entrepreneur they aim to act upon and to constitute. What is important to hold in mind, is the different though interconnected political histories and realities behind the economic exclusion and distress that lead particular social groups to become a constituency for empowerment interventions.

Drawing on the work of Barbara Cruikshank (1999) on empowerment and self-help programmes as a technology of citizenship, I take interest in the productive power of intervention programmes designed by and for women, particularly for women on the margins of citizenship. Cruickshank offers to analyse empowerment as constituting in itself a relationship of power between the empowering and the empowered, between institutions and practitioners and their constituencies. This technology aims to engineer empowered and entrepreneurial citizens who act upon their wills and interests—but it also aspires to construct these very wills and interests. The main question of this chapter is, which gendered entrepreneurial citizens this field works to produce, and how? How can we understand the project to educate and enterprise women as entrepreneurs and entrepreneurial subjects as a political project of subject-making? Which epistemological normative assumptions are enacted in the process of enterprising the entrepreneurs, of constructing the gendered entrepreneurial self?

We encounter assumptions about entrepreneurship, proper economic and social conduct, gender roles, balance of family and work, private and public sphere, race and ethnicity, all enacted in the process. I am particularly interested in how the field of women's economic empowerment—via its institutions and practitioners—perceives and constructs the participants, their needs, strengths and weaknesses, and the process they need to go through, in order to reach the desired destination: to become an empowered woman entrepreneur. Of course, this is not a straightforward process; programmes aiming to re-engineer participants in certain ways do not necessarily work like magic. They do not always meet their goals, stated or implicit; women participating in these programmes do not necessarily end up in the destination envisioned for them by empowerment programmes and their practitioners. Women's agency is central here, and in fact, many of the discourses and practices of the field are made visible precisely through women's ambivalence or outright resistance towards certain requirements and assumptions of the entrepreneurial training process. Likewise, examining empowerment and entrepreneurship training as a technology of citizenship does not automatically assume or imply that this technology functions seamlessly in any given time and place. Methodologically, our discussion zooms in on the relations and interactions between civil society organisations and their constituencies: how practitioners and participants manage and negotiate their relations and the activities they engage in, and how they perceive and narrate the processes of empowerment and entrepreneurial training, both in the course of their formal activities and informal communication. And, to begin with, how do they perceive the constituencies they aim to benefit, how do they perceive and interpret their needs and interests?

There is little resemblance between the lived realities of marginalised women of all ages who turn to micro-entrepreneurship out of necessity and lack of (suitable) alternatives, and the mythic image of the risk-taking, young and spirited entrepreneur following his dream and effortlessly mobilising personal and economic resources for its realisation. Necessity-driven entrepreneurship inevitably clashes with the ethos of entrepreneurship as a voluntary expression of an inner drive for innovation and success, and calls for a fundamental redefinition of entrepreneurial activities and entrepreneurial identities. In examining the distinctive aspects of entrepreneurship that is necessity-driven, I centre the agency of the participants. We shall see that the participants are active in redefining what entrepreneurship is, and what it can be, through their participation and engagement with discourses and practices in the field—complicity with and acceptance of some, resistance to and rejection of others.

Still, let us begin with the classic representations of the entrepreneur that largely continue dominating popular imagery—not just of the public, but also in policy-making. A self-employed immigrant woman in Berlin recalled a politician who commented on the phenomena of entrepreneurs earning too little to meet the extensive payments and insurances required by German law: "There was this issue that some small entrepreneurs earned too little to pay these [heath and other insurances], and then there was some conservative politician who said, somebody who earns that little, shouldn't be entrepreneur. So the notion was clearly that entrepreneur is someone who earns a lot of money, who has capital. So this is entrepreneur in the sense that he [the politician] understands." Such messages signal clearly that micro-entrepreneurs are falling short of the popular normative image of the entrepreneur. This conservative politician voiced a rather common view on entrepreneurship, and the norm for who can be—and should be—an entrepreneur. The perception of the entrepreneur as a person managing a large-scale firm still dominates the public imagery (Bührmann, 2010).

Why is the normative image of the entrepreneur at all important? Symbolic realms, images and representations bear material consequences and concrete effects on social and economic life. The impact of the normative entrepreneurial image cannot be underrated. It influences individual's self-perception and one's decision whether to embark on the path or entrepreneurship. It guides NGO practitioners in comprehending and defining the needs of their target groups and designing the services for them. Finally, it underlies the thinking and the conduct of the lawmaker designing policies, the bureaucrat implementing them, and the bank clerk deciding to approve or reject a request for a loan made by the person in front of them. In the classic liberal imagery, entrepreneurship is a meritocratic and profit-oriented economic activity performed by the universal rational subject, one that is motivated by self-interest and the drive for innovation and success. The entrepreneur is constructed after the iconic image of *homo economics* coined by the early economists, who have envisioned a rational subject acting upon his self-interest (Anderson, 2000; Tedmanson et al., 2012). This classic envisioning of the entrepreneur as an exceptional individual can also be traced to the early influential theorist of entrepreneurship, Joseph Schumpeter, in his 1911 *The Theory of Economic Development*. The Schumpeterian entrepreneur still maintains hold on the popular imagination and its practical manifestations in legislation and policy, although Schumpeter himself, in his later economic theory, has de-personalised his concepts of entrepreneurship and innovation. He effectively shifted from centring the individual to a more historicised view of processes and institutions—yet, this shift was not favourably received in the scientific milieu of economists, and his earlier work maintained its hold (Śledzik, 2013).

In the tradition of liberalism, this envisioning of a universal subject omits social identity markers as race and ethnicity, gender and class. In contrast, a sociological perspective underscores that society is more than an assemblage of universal rational subjects; it is comprised of social groups enjoying highly differentiated economic, social and cultural capital in their access to entrepreneurial resources and in their resemblance to the image of the entrepreneur. In this vein, critical entrepreneurship literature points to the "limitations upon the possibilities of who can claim the subject position of 'entrepreneur'" (Ahl & Marlow, 2012: 544). Individuals from marginalised communities are likely to deviate from the normative entrepreneurial image because of their gender, ethnic and class background, their motivations and the range of resources at their disposal. Even the individuals that are more affluent do not ideally correspond to the classic image of the entrepreneur, or *homo economics* at large. The traditional areas of literature on entrepreneurship increasingly explore questions of shame and insecurity, fear of failure, and other emotional factors made invisible by the heroic narratives of the risk-taking entrepreneur making his first million by sheer talent, business-savvy and determination. Scholars increasingly recognise that in the real world, people do not always behave rationally, nor are they merely self-interested individuals making rational decisions based on cost-effectiveness. However, not all forms of deviation from the norm equally disqualify an individual from claiming this entrepreneurial subject position.

Marginalised women taking on the entrepreneurial path constantly face their nonconformity to the entrepreneurial image. They encounter this imagery as it is reflected in legal and policy definitions, in professional discourses, in popular culture and in widespread cultural perceptions among their own family and friends. They encounter it in conflicting demands from their business and from their family and community. This deviation from the image of the entrepreneur positions them as the 'other' and differentiates them from normative entrepreneurial goals and motivations, identities and personalities, lifestyles and family arrangements. This otherness is intrinsically related to gender norms and their associated division of domestic labour, intersecting with ethnicity and socio-economic class, among possible other factors. And, this otherness is visible not only to the women themselves, but, as I shall demonstrate, also to the practitioners and institutional actors around them, and it is ingrained in their practices. At the same time, if earlier critique pointed out the exclusionary image of the entrepreneur, today women and immigrants are no longer absent from entrepreneurship research or its public imagery. They are still greatly under-represented—in policy, media and research. Yet, as images of the immigrant entrepreneur or the female entrepreneur increasingly surface in policy documents, media items and in entrepreneurship research, the critical task is not solely to measure their mere presence, but to examine their content, possibilities and limitations.

I begin by sketching the diverse constituencies of ISI e.V. and AEEW, and proceed to contrasting them with entrepreneurial imagery. Drawing on examples from the EU, Germany and Israel, I consider two spheres of entrepreneurial image construction—legal definitions and female role models—and examine its relevance to immigrant and low-income women. In comparison, Germany and Israel exemplify profoundly different legal-administrative, political and economic contexts for entrepreneurship. Comparative examination of their legal and administrative regulations and requirements from the perspective of immigrant and low-income women effectively shows that the entrepreneurial image assumed by each of these frameworks is incompatible with women's lives, experiences, possibilities and needs. It also reveals how this incompatibility plays out differently in each national context. The first evident and explicit answer to the question 'who can be entrepreneur' is found in its legal definition and legal requirements for business registration. Policies and their associated definitions and requirements express the recognition given by the state or the municipal authority to certain economic activities and those performing them. It is evident that entrepreneurship policies and regulations in countries like Germany and Israel were designed in an era when the vast majority of population was expected to rely on traditional employment. In many countries, national associations of micro-business owners and the self-employed protest the incompatibility of policy frameworks and advocate for policy adjustments to reflect their actual needs and their contribution to economic growth. Both German and Israeli associations speak in highly critical terms of state policies and regulations, presenting the micro-entrepreneurs and the self-employed as helpless in front of unreasonable policies and bureaucratic hardships. These difficulties multiply in necessity-driven entrepreneurship and add to the precariousness of marginalised groups, lacking financial safety nets and alternative employment opportunities.

In Germany, the bureaucratic and administrative workload and the burden of multiple insurance payments on micro-entrepreneurs are often experienced as disproportional to the actual income and profit of the small business. In the words of an interviewee, a self-employed educated woman with migration family history: "I think self-employment is a complex thing. It gives you the freedom of deciding what you do, of feeling creative, and on the other hand, you are permanently under pressure to actually get, to earn enough money, and that might be interesting, the whole regulations around self-employment in Germany are very much around the idea of earning much more money than people like me do, because the minimum rate for some of the, for health insurance, are really high. [...] So the regulations around self-employment are the way you can't really survive as a low-income self-employed entrepreneur. The regulations are all thinking of some creative marketing whatever or Steuerberater [tax consultant] who wants to smuggle money around from taxation office because they think, he must be earning more than he is telling us." Such subjective accounts of disproportional administrative and financial overload are matched by official evaluations of the entrepreneurial environment, although these reports do not specifically contrast the burden of health and other insurances on an individual with humble earnings. It is important to note that some areas are significantly more burdensome in terms of administration and bureaucracy than others: for obvious reasons, a bakery or another gastronomy business generally requires a great deal more paperwork and permits than business consulting, graphic design or other knowledge-based service provision. EU's 2014 SBA (Small Business Act) Fact Sheet on Germany praises the overall performance of enterprises in Germany and the good business conditions for existing firms, but criticises the conditions for start-up—access to finance and the administrative procedures. Measuring Germany's variation from the EU for 2011, on "Licenses and permit systems" (1 = lowest level of complexity, 26 =

highest level of complexity), Germany scored 21.2 in relation to the European average of 15.77. Complicated license and permit systems are particularly burdensome for micro-entrepreneurs with limited time on their hands, for instance, caregivers in their families, and for those with limited resources, like imperfect command of German language, or as termed by one interviewee—"bureaucratic German", that is often unclear even to the native German speakers.

In Israel, practitioners have repeatedly stated in the interviews that low-income women in micro-entrepreneurship are generally "beyond the radar" of the relevant authorities, such as the Authority for Small and Medium Businesses under the Ministry of Economy. An interview I conducted in the Authority itself further corroborates this statement. The exceptions are minor, although they do exist: such is the current cooperation between the Authority and the microcredit provider KIEDF, offering loans and business consulting to Arab women. In fact, micro-businesses as such are simply not in the centre of the Authority's agenda, and it is only in recent years that they began receiving more attention. Since 2008, the Authority conducts an entrepreneurship training programme Yozmim Esek ("initiating a business" in Hebrew) designed for the unemployed and for those defined as "special populations", including Palestinians (recognised by Israel as Arabs, not as Palestinians), ultra-Orthodox Jews, immigrants, single mothers, young adults in the periphery and, most recently, people released after serving a prison sentence. This colourful mix of social groups brings about the concern that entrepreneurship is serving to "bypass" structural problems of the labour market, instead of developing solutions within the framework of traditional employment. Problems such as lack of jobs in the periphery, work culture that is unfriendly to single parents, overt or hidden discrimination against ethnic and religious minorities, and social stigmatisation of former prisoners. Simply put, this message can be understood as—if nobody is willing to employ you, employ yourself.

The limited attention given to micro-entrepreneurs is surprising, in light of the fact that the vast majority of the businesses in Israel, as in Germany, are micro-businesses. This can be explained, firstly, by the relatively high rates of entrepreneurship in Israel—unlike Germany, where the rates are lower than desirable for the national agenda. In Germany as in Europe generally, there is an explicit national and regional interest to encourage potential entrepreneurs for national economic development, on top of its potential to reduce unemployment and serve as an alternative to providing more opportunities of traditional employment to marginalised populations. The legal definition of small and micro enterprise also sheds some light on the gap between policy and reality, pointing out again to the influential role of normative assumptions. The Authority defines small business as one that employs up to 19 employees and has annual turnover up to 20 million ILS, while micro-business employs up to 4 employees with an annual turnover of up to 1 million ILS (Israeli definitions differ from the EU standard, according to which micro-business employs 0–9 employees, and small business 10–50 employees). Yet, over 50% of all businesses in Israel employed only the owner, while micro-businesses with 1–4 employees comprise approximately one-third of all businesses. Thus, while micro-businesses employing only the owner are the majority of the businesses in the country, practitioners have noted with dissatisfaction that such micro-businesses are not properly defined, and subsequently are not provided with suitable services.

Israeli policy and welfare frameworks entail particular hardships for people relying on welfare at the outset of their entrepreneurial activity–a profile valid for many women served by NGOs like AEEW and Supportive Environment (which meanwhile no longer exists). I have found social justice and women's economic empowerment organisations to be unanimous in their ambivalent approach to the path of policy change, due to their mixed experience: investment of enormous resources versus what they assess to be as very humble gains. This position was reached the hard way, upon conducting several battles on legal and policy-making grounds, in order to counter structural obstacles facing marginalised women on their path to becoming entrepreneurs. One such major battle took place in Israel in 2008 around the policies of the National Insurance Institute, which required a person to show evidence of income in early stages of the business. Otherwise, in order to keep the guaranteed minimal income, the person was sent to the employment centre and possibly placed in a workplace, hence not being able to invest that much needed time in actually starting the business. Although the NGOs involved in this battle were successful in changing the regulations, this change was not properly implemented. Clerks in local offices were not aware of the new regulations or disregarded them, and the revisited regulations were eventually dropped. Interviewees observe that it required vast investment of time and energy resources from the NGOs, whilst the gain was minimal. This ambivalence reflects the prevailing attitude in many Israeli civil society organisations towards institutional change: They continue engaging with state institutions, refusing out of principle to give it up as a path for change, while maintaining high scepticism of the actual viability of this change to come about. The immediate outcome of these hardships is the refrainment of women micro-entrepreneurs from registering their business—essentially, their refrainment from becoming entrepreneurs in the legal sense of this category. Practitioners observe this practice with empathy and understand this de facto illegal economic activity as a grey area, gently defining it as informal economy. The Economic Justice Clinic of Tel Aviv University's Faculty of Law provided a significant deal of its legal services to women who have not registered their business. Microfinance providers also approved loans to non-registered businesses, although they tend to pressure their clients to register their businesses as soon as possible, for instance by including it as a condition for a second loan.

While the widespread image of the entrepreneur is still marked by membership in the hegemonic group, women and immigrants are no longer absent, but rather allocated a specific place in the entrepreneurial sphere. In Germany, a discourse analysis of the entrepreneurial image in main websites of entrepreneurship consultancy and support has shown that both women and immigrants are still perceived and constructed as "others", differing from the normative image of the entrepreneur (Bührmann, 2010: 61). This difference was found with regard to entrepreneurial motivation, development and goals, as well as in relation to economic, cultural and social capital, and to the presence of so-called entrepreneurial personality, indeed the celebrated entrepreneurial self. Researchers found that professional discourses surrounding women and immigrants in entrepreneurship perceive them as less goal-oriented and strategic than the "normative" entrepreneur. Instead, women and immigrants were seen as forced into entrepreneurship by unemployment and circumstances. They were also perceived as lacking economic and cultural capital, and family appeared as a source of support for men, and a source of responsibility for women. We thus see women and migrants trapped between two binary representations: the unrealistic classical image of the driven and excited risk-taking entrepreneur, with its white, wealthy and masculine bias, and the stereotypical image of the "other", the flawed entrepreneur—lacking drive and creativity, forced by circumstances, burdened by their kin ties and commitments.

Representations of successful women entrepreneurs are deliberately created as a strategy to increase the number of women in entrepreneurship. In 2009, the European Commission's Directorate-General for

Enterprise and Industry inaugurated The European Network of Female Entrepreneurship Ambassadors. The initiative builds on EC's earlier efforts, such as The European Network to Promote Women's Entrepreneurship (WES). The purpose of the Female Entrepreneurship Ambassadors' Network is to provide women in Europe with female role models to inspire, encourage and assist them to become entrepreneurs. The Network targets women facing different forms of difficulty in the labour market and in traditional employment, from fresh graduates to women returning from parental leave. Its target audiences include "women from different backgrounds, in particular unemployed women, students and female university graduates, working women with an interest and potential to set up their own business, women returning from a baby break, women working with and/or interested in innovation, manufacturing and research and development". The absence of factors like migration history, race/ethnicity, religion, class or other identity factors are quite telling. The terminology and the visual language of the network draw a picture of a collective of well-educated women in fields associated with middle and upper class rather than lower socio-economic status professions. The network is intended for women to relate to the Ambassadors' life stories on an interpersonal level, resulting in an increased sense of self-confidence, motivation and chances of success. The capacity of women in the target audience to relate to and to identify with the Ambassadors is clearly integral to the network's success. Yet, lack of implicit or explicit attention to national, ethnic and class inequalities among women makes it difficult to assess who eventually are the women relating to these stories, and no less important, who are the women who cannot relate.

The practice of networking itself is also worth a moment of attention. Social networking has been ascribed to the entrepreneur already in its early Schumpeterian conceptualisation (Davies, 2016: 53). Over the decades, the practice of networking has undergone transformations in content and format and received varying degrees of research interest. However, its impact on the world of labour in general, and business in particular, is undisputed. In recent years, a call is made to women to embrace the practice of networking, in order to advance their careers and overcome inequalities in the labour market. This call can be found in best-sellers of recent years, such as Sheryl Sandberg's *Lean In: Women, Work, and the Will to Lead*, possibly the best-known representative book of neoliberal feminism (Rottenberg, 2014). Women's exclusion from the old boys' club and women's own reluctance to lean in are explained as one of the factors reinforcing women's inferior position in business culture. Angela McRobbie notes in her discussion of Sheryl Sandberg's Lean In that "...there is a whole vocabulary which describes the world of non-elite labour which is totally missing from her writing. This includes such words as poverty and unemployment, the high cost and often low quality of childcare, the reliance of white, middle-class, elite women on the low-paid domestic labour of migrant women, many of whom will be separated from their own children in order to earn a living and hence unable themselves to provide "quality parenting", and so on" (McRobbie, 2013: 135). Although Sandberg and other authors associated with neoliberal feminism bring forth the practice of networking among women as a parallel form to the old boys' club, McRobbie insists that this networking is clearly delineated by boundaries of socio-economic class and remains within capitalist value systems, specifically profit and competition. I suggest that these are precisely the boundaries of socio-economic class that allow the initiatives like the Female Entrepreneurship Ambassadors Network to term entrepreneurship as lifestyle and to promote it as a privileged arrangement that promises meritocracy and a better work–life balance. The vocabulary describing the experiences of marginalised women who form the constituency of women's economic empowerment organisations like AEEW and ISI e.V. is clearly absent from the manifesto of the Ambassadors and similar celebrations of female entrepreneurship.

What would such a vocabulary look like? For example, this is how Yaara, a woman who worked as an art-director for an advertising agency, and then turned to be an observant religious Jew, explains her turn to entrepreneurship in an interview to the Israeli online daily *Ynet*: "Because I was a single mother for about seven years, and I lived from guaranteed minimal income [havtahat hachnasa], in the employment agency they wanted to send me to clean toilets and kitchens in hospitals. Exactly then they opened in Mati Bnei-Brak a course of 'Business of One's Own' of the Association for the Economic Empowerment for Women, and they explained me that if you register to the course, you can escape this destiny. Of course I registered, and I learned how to be an entrepreneur [...] from then on my star rose high." Although ultimately told as a narrative of success, Yaara's story illuminates the lives of women for whom the turn to entrepreneurship has been a matter of economic survival, necessity, or pressure under punitive social policies and harsh market economy, rather than a new lifestyle, a search for a more meritocratic sphere or a pursuit of the optimal work–life balance. Indeed, the discourse on entrepreneurship as a guarantee of meritocracy for women overlooks structural inequalities of the market—for women in general, and for women experiencing multiple and intersecting forms of oppression in particular. Discourses promoted by networks and initiatives such as this frame entrepreneurship as a lifestyle, as a pathway to a better work—life balance, as a priority for policymakers. "We believe that entrepreneurship gives women a guarantee of a real meritocracy, frequently denied in many sectors of business and politics", reads the Network's mission statement. While this discourse constructs women's entrepreneurship as the greener, environmentally friendlier and overall nicer version of the general business culture, the structural inequalities characterising it remain beyond scope. Initiatives as the Female Ambassadors Network are well understood in the neoliberal context of maintaining market-driven focus while generously incorporating concepts of social justice and gender equality. Here, the emphasis on personal resources and confidence building enables privatising objective and structural problems in society and economy, reducing them to dependence on a woman's individual personality and ambition. This, in itself, is also in full compatibility with the project of neoliberal governance.

The family is a particularly evident sphere where social expectations from women and from entrepreneurs may fundamentally clash with each other. The classic image of the entrepreneur as a singular and exceptional figure stands in relative isolation from the family. Of course, this isolation is only made possible by the gendered traditional division of productive and reproductive labour as separate masculine and feminine spheres. Women's reproductive labour, including domestic labour and care for children and the elderly, while publicly invisible and devalued, nonetheless serves to support and enable the existence of the productive labour as we know it. When women entrepreneurs come to embody both productive and reproductive labour, they experience first-hand the construction of these spheres as oppositional to each other. As noted, professional discourses of entrepreneurship construct the family as a source of support for male entrepreneurs, and a source of responsibility for female entrepreneurs and for immigrant entrepreneurs (Bührmann, 2010). The capacity of the family to function as a source of support is not as self-evident for women: it is not a given, but rather an achievement to be won. Soliciting the support of the partner and negotiating with family members is often integrated in women's economic empowerment curriculums. In a thank-you letter addressed to AEEW, one of its participants, Gila Halag, wrote: "[M]y main problem at that time was my inability to by physically present with my husband in the business, even though professionally and in terms of division of roles we manage it was alright. I was looking all the time for what is wrong and why it does not work out. After about 3 months in the course and with the help of the trainers, I understood that the working space in its current form physically does not suffice for both of us – I have no place to sit! I am telling all this because without the course I would not have come to this simple realisation." For Gila and many other participants, a process of personal empowerment, economic independence, and a combination of the two, provide the psychosocial space to reconsider their family life, to assess and challenge gender roles in the family, or to leave their partner altogether. As Amalia Sa'ar (2014) notes, economic empowerment courses facilitate access for low-income women to cultural practices of the middle class, where they can adopt reflexive emotional speech and embrace narratives of self-reliance.

High percentage of divorce among the participants is characteristic of women's empowerment participants, and came up in many of the interviews I have conducted with practitioners. Some practitioners brought up the subject with notions of shy humour and embarrassment, as if they were caught doing something wrong. This story told by an ISI e.V. employee is an example: "We also had negative cases, when two men took their wives out of our course, because they became rather self-confident. Occasionally taking a stand against something. We struggled against it for a long time, but did not manage. And generally it is astounding that divorce is quite common for these women (the participants). I sometimes say, we should somehow close our business down (laughing); it is precisely because they achieve financial independence, precisely because they are more certain of their own strength, and then they of course think, well, alright, that's it, I am now leaving this patriarch." Even NGOs like Supportive Environment in Israel, which focused solely on economic empowerment and avoided explicitly feminist contents and mission statements, found themselves facing the problem of domestic violence. These problems simply came up when women talked about their lives, and could not be ignored. In response, the organisation decided to include contents in their programme to "strengthen the family" while also directing women suffering domestic violence to appropriate services for support.

Women also report difficulties charging relatives and acquaintances for their services. This is a major problem for rural women, when their primary or indeed the only clientele is their immediate community and their village. Relatives and acquaintances often feel entitled to free services, discounts and endlessly belated payments, making market-based financial conduct difficult to impossible. Sa'ar in her ethnography also reviews various strategies developed by the women to cope with these challenges, such as keeping their income and financial situation in secrecy—at times even from their spouses. The relatives' sense of entitlement is one way to interpret the situation. Another way is the existence of community economies less subjected to individualistic calculations of profit, where people are accustomed to communal networks of care, support and service provision, albeit these networks tend to depend on the undervalued labour of women. The need to renegotiate expectations from the relatives and the community sets a price tag and recognition on the labour, but also extends market logics and practices into communities on the margins of the formal economy.

Neoliberalism traps women simultaneously in market logics and in traditional family roles and expectations. While economic empowerment and entrepreneurship programmes train their participants to adopt some of the self-interested entrepreneurial attitude, women are still expected to invest their income and profits into the well-being of their families. This is in contrast to the neoliberal image of the universal self-centred individual acting in his own self-interest—the prototype of the entrepreneur, whose family may be seen as his extension or as beneficiaries of his gains, but it is certainly not a site of primary investment of funds over business growth and his own entrepreneurial aspirations and pursuits. Women may seem as the exception to the neoliberal logic. In effect, these gender norms are central to neoliberalism, in that they mobilise women to function as a safety net for their families against the impoverishing impacts of neoliberal macroeconomic policies on marginalised communities.

Let us now take a closer look at curriculums of personal and economic empowerment to examine the actual process of becoming an entrepreneur. Women's economic empowerment and entrepreneurship training organisations cope with the gap between classical entrepreneurial representation and the life realities of women participating in empowerment programmes in a dual way. First, they aim to bring women closer to resemble the entrepreneurial image. This is where empowerment emerges most strongly as a relationship of power, by which its target group is defined in terms of lack and deficiency, and offered concrete directions for personal transformation. Second, they challenge the normative assumptions of entrepreneurial activity and aim to produce diverse models, such as those combining business and family. In other words, they aim to "adjust" marginalised women to fit entrepreneurial image, and to "adjust" the entrepreneurial image to fit marginalised women.

A comparative overview of entrepreneurship training curriculums indicates the depth of intervention that these programmes aim to achieve. The programmes do not only instruct the participants how to act, they also instruct how to be. For example, one of ISI e.V. four pillars in the entrepreneurship-training programme is "nurturing an entrepreneurial personality". An element of personal transformative change through a range of psychodynamic activities is characteristic of empowerment and entrepreneurship training programmes, although its form and volume differ from one curriculum to another. Naturally, all curriculums offer formal entrepreneurial education: business plan development, assessment of market needs and opportunities, basic accounting and bookkeeping, tax regulations, marketing skills and so on. Some curriculums include outright explicit elements of personal empowerment: this is especially characteristic of organisations grounded in feminist and social justice ideologies. For instance, AEEW's entrepreneurship training programme ascribes two facilitators to each group of participants: one for personal empowerment and one for economic empowerment. Other programmes assume empowerment to be incorporated in the entrepreneurial process and in improving one's own economic situation. This assumption is common in the development industry and among organisations whose self-identification, overall approach and organisational discourse are less explicitly feminist and political. For organisations like Supportive Environment, the key indicator of success was increasing income. The rationale, as explained to me by one practitioner who didn't identify as feminist, is that focusing on a great deal of personal or political matters is confusing and wastes resources, while focusing on breaking the barrier of income leads to improvement in other spheres of life as well.

However, even those organisations that do not allocate designated content units and human resources to personal empowerment, involve a range of educational contents concerning one's way of being, such as time-management, communication skills and intercultural communication. Moreover, as mentioned, they could not escape realities of women's lives, such as domestic violence and low self-esteem. As a co-founder of Supportive Environment said, with a notion of parody: "[a woman could say] I charge less because people don't think I'm worthy and my father was violent. [Our approach is:] We can't take care of the father, but let's see how from this starting point of you being worthy, you can start charging more money [for your products/services]. [We communicate the message that] you can give discounts only when you make money. You can volunteer in your business when there is money. When it is a choice." Here, transformation of economic conduct is acknowledged as a tool for increasing a woman's self-esteem, by increasing the financial and emotional value of her labour.

In order to be relevant to women's lives, micro-entrepreneurship is constructed very differently from the entrepreneurial ethos. It is reconstructed in a way that makes it relevant to their lives but at the same time distances it from the original entrepreneurial claim to profit and power. As Sa'ar finds, women in NGOs like AEEW do not aim to "make money" and they are also not encouraged to do so by the professional discourses around them; she notes, with a hint of irony, that the women are expected to earn "something". ISI e.V. with its seemingly slightly more educated and well-off constituency, eventually also strives for basic economic independence for women, rather than them "making money". The participants might indeed be sceptical about "making money" and outright resist letting go of their way of life, even when according to the practitioners that makes business sense. AEEW practitioner reported a difficult and frustrating learning experience, when their attempt to open a co-working space for micro-entrepreneurs in the old city of Acre failed: "We opened a greenhouse in Acre. That was after our consultants worked with women, and they saw that a woman who works in the old Acre, small homes, the families are quite traditional Arab, she wants to run a hairdressing business, if her husband is at home, she cannot let her client in. That is, the conditions are terribly problematic, to run the business from home. So we said, let's solve this problem for them. Let's take the business, create a space, where she could come. We ran after the women, first we said that they can pay a symbolic fee of 200 shekels, then we said they can have it for free, because we didn't want to hold an empty space. Women didn't want to come. They didn't want to come. They're used to it, living this way. How to do this change, we didn't manage that, in my opinion. I don't know how they do it in other places." Low-income women of ethnic minorities, in establishing and operating a business, face a great deal of challenges. Lack of access to credit, traditional division of gender roles, social and cultural norms and habits, are but a few of the challenges. "We didn't manage that" admits the practitioner, but this is a difficult responsibility to take—changing gender roles and social order is not a task for one organisation only. Becoming an entrepreneur is more compatible with some forms of social life, and less compatible with others. Not everyone is required to fundamentally alter their spatial habits, and to be absent from home when this absence might undermine the social capital they have acquired in their domestic role, especially if there are limited forms of social capital available to them. This, I suggest, is a side effect of micro-entrepreneurship allowing women to build on the social capital they already have. In traditional communities, where women's social capital derives from their domestic position, they might not be eager letting go of it for a promise of a different future. We can thus see the inherent complexity of entrepreneurship as a solution for women's social and economic exclusion. The distinctively masculine, white and middle-upper-class bias of entrepreneurship as a practice, and entrepreneur as a subject position, positions all others—women, immigrants, ethnic minorities, people in poverty—as failed, reluctant or deviant entrepreneurs, who require "fixing" in order to fit in. Yet, there is no guarantee that this is at all possible.

To illustrate the dynamic process designed to construct the entrepreneurial self, I highlight several aspects from the curriculum of AEEW and its concrete contents, exercises, and activities. One of the first sessions in the entrepreneurship training programme is titled "awareness of personal resources" and is fascinating in its explicit intervention with one's own self-perception. In the first exercise, each woman needs to write 15 traits and qualities she possesses, which could serve her in the economic sphere; women discuss those traits with each other, and then discuss the qualities necessary for a woman entrepreneur. Here, women's low self-esteem and lack of awareness of their personal resources is taken for granted as a starting point in this exercise, and in the entrepreneurship training programme at large. The psychodynamic process entails elements of self-reflection on one's own qualities, proceeding to reflection through peer contact and group activity. These preliminary stages are designed to assist women to overcome the difficulty to account for their own qualities and acknowledge them to themselves and to others.

The second exercise requires each participant to imagine her birthday in five years, and two people from her family and work life describing her to the guests. Participants need to compare these descriptions with their own lists from the first exercise. This second exercise confronts women with possible gaps between their own self-perception, and the way they are seen—and wish to be seen—by others. This exercise again assumes low self-esteem, and the purpose is to help the participants see that an external (possibly more "objective") opinion of them is higher than their own. Their own self-perception is relativised, and this relativism is again offered to the participants for a reflexive assessment.

Finally, the participants are introduced to a Hebrew-language poem "Ima" (mom) by Iris Eliya Cohen, a daughter to immigrants from the Jewish community of Cochin, India—a Mizrahi woman, like some of the participants. This poem is a testimony of a daughter about her hardworking mother, whose care and domestic labour has gone unrecognised. She describes her mother's day, filled with endless tasks and on her feet all day, and yet when asked what her parents do, the daughter would reply "mommy doesn't work". The poem may resonate with the lived experience of many women from the constituency catered by AEEW, and with that of their own mothers. It invokes a critical and somewhat ironic perspective on social norms that fail to recognise women's reproductive and domestic labour as "work", and, it is followed by a closing round of summary, thoughts and insights the participants are invited to share. This is an explicit moment where the capitalist definition of work is in fact challenged, and an empowering space for recognising reproductive and care labour is created.

The exercises and the poem come together in framing the shared experience of the women in the group in the larger and multi-generational story of women in society. This recalls classical feminist methods of consciousness-raising, serving to show that problems taken to be personal are in fact common, and originate in societal structures which oppress women individually and collectively. There is one more, optional, activity for that session. The facilitator distributes to the participants a sheet with a list of affirmation statements, a marker and a notebook. The participants write in the notebook statements from the list, which they agree to repeat every morning and evening. Statements like "my life is full of love and joy", "I deserve all the good that exists", "I speak my mind without fear". Repetition is a powerful practice, and its strong religious connotations recall a prayer. It is a common tool for self-help programmes like addiction recovery. This list, with its rather new-age aura, entails some utterances that are far from being self-evident for women. "I speak my mind without fear" can be a subversive statement for many participants, who live in an environment where they and their opinions are undervalued and where domestic violence prevails. Another session of the programme aims at promoting assertive conduct. In this exercise, women engage in simulations in pairs: they simulate a business conversation and the participant has to say each message in three different ways: assertive, aggressive and passive. The simulations are followed by a group discussion on why it is so hard for women to be assertive. As with empowerment, the activities in this session assume that women lack assertiveness, that it is particularly hard for women to be assertive and that it goes against gendered norms of upbringing. This intervention takes place on the level of motivation, of emotional reaction and of practical conduct. Simulated situations include, among others: "A client has accumulated a debt of 1,000 NIS. You need the money. She is coming to your business. What do you tell her?"; "You need money urgently. Ask a friend to lend you 1,000 NIS"; "Ask a person who sits too close to you on the bus to move." This exercise directs participants and practitioners alike to comprehend this activity as a discovery and expression of that pre-existing inner voice, a primal subjectivity that liberates itself from anxiety, from fears, from complying with repression and denial of personal rights. However, and this is the main argument here, these guiding questions "what do you tell her?", "how do you react?" can and perhaps should be read as "what should you be telling her?", "how should you be reacting?" They serve a clear instructional purpose and imply from the outset how should the entrepreneurial subject be speaking and acting. In other words, these training activities manifest a technology that empowers participants to act on their wills and interests, but also serves to construct and communicate what these wills and interests should be.

Technologies of self-help and personal empowerment have been criticised by many feminist theorists and activists for their presumably depoliticising effect. Barbra Cruikshank (1999) recalls that books such as Gloria Steinem's *Revolution from Within: A Book of Self-Esteem* were accused of shifting the feminist focus from the public to the private sphere. The focus on individual well-being and self-esteem, this critique implies, comes at the expense of collective action for social and political change. However, self-esteem is very much political. One's relation to oneself is always-already a product of social relations and political order. Self-esteem and empowerment programmes do politicise personal life, turning one's own self-perception and consciousness into a terrain of political intervention and action. As Cruikshank notes, this is not necessarily recognised by self-esteem advocates like Steinem. They may assume an inner voice, a true self, some sort of a primal subjectivity that precedes repression. Thus, both self-esteem advocates and their critics may fail to account for "the extent to which the citizen is (like inequality, poverty and racism) the product of power relations, the outcome of strategies and technologies developed to create everything from autonomy and empowerment to self-help" (1999: 103). In her own ethnography of AEEW, Amalia Sa'ar finds that personal empowerment sessions effectively respond to women's needs for personal development and growth. Drawing on the work of Eva Illouz, Sa'ar notes that reflexivity and personal development are central to the modern notion of freedom. Low-income women cannot afford the expensive activities of psychological therapy, coaching, self-discovery and various individual enlightenment and new-age practices, generally consumed by middle-class women and men. Curriculums of empowerment that combine this element allow for participation in such middle-class consumerist practices. Sa'ar notes with irony the paradoxical nature of this personal empowerment: it may raise the participants' self-esteem, but at the same time strengthen the liberal social order that marginalises them in the first place. The rhetoric of empowerment implies an individual that requires "fixing", omitting how this low self-esteem came about. These curriculums clearly acknowledge that low self-esteem is a product of external forces, which can and should be reversed with a set of practices. But can increasing the participants' self-esteem truly alter these structures or to counter these forces?

Consciousness-raising is a method embraced as radical, emancipatory and transformative by feminist movements, applied in various interventions to alter the self, and incorporated in the process of economic empowerment and entrepreneurship training. Given its centrality in the globalisation of feminism and in the production of entrepreneurial subjectivities, I offer an explanation to account for its survival and its transformation, as it lands in the programmes of economic empowerment. Though often associated with the history of second-wave feminism in the West, the method of consciousness-raising has also been highly prominent in the global South. Primarily in Latin America and South Asia, feminists approached empowerment through consciousness-raising. Since the 1970s, through the method of consciousness-raising women have identified commonalities in their lived experiences and became aware of structural conditions and mechanisms of their oppression in both public and private spheres. Consciousness-raising was revolutionary for the unprecedented forms of globalisation of second-wave feminism. It is of relevance to empowerment, because it shows how the individual experience and individual transformation of consciousness has been most fundamental for the feminist movement. Feminist geographers and authors of an original feminist critique of capitalism, JK Gibson-Graham (1997), speak with admiration of this unimaginable success of a global movement without managers, although at times and places with coordination and connections. "The complex intermixing of alternative discourses, shared language, embodied practices, self-cultivation, emplaced actions, and global transformation associated with second-wave feminist has nourished our thinking about a politics of economic possibility—impressing us with the simple ontological contours of a feminist imaginary: if women are everywhere, a woman is always somewhere, and those places are transformed as women transform themselves."

We speak of the contemporary neoliberal move from the collective to the individual level as a problematic process. Yet in the earlier practices of consciousness-raising, the individual subject was present and central. What has changed is the relation of the individual subject to society, the substance of transformation taking place in her consciousness, and the implications and outcomes of the consciousness-raising process: namely no more the need for social change and collective transformation. In other words, when Western second-wave feminists said that the personal is political, they did not mean to say that political is only in the personal. This is precisely the turning point in the re-organisation of relations among the personal and the political that has accompanied the neoliberal stage in the transformation of the consciousness-raising method, and its integration in economic empowerment and entrepreneurship training. In line with the neoliberal spirit, the political has been reduced to the personal.

I have found women's economic empowerment organisations to shy away from outcomes of empowerment that might lead to conflict and confrontation—"assertiveness" practiced in the personal empowerment curriculum was not intended to translate to outrage at racial or gender discrimination and to political organising. In a way, practitioners invest efforts to contain the changes generated by their own activities. For Western second-wave feminist theorists like Catherine McKinnon, consciousness-raising is the feminist method for women to know and comprehend their own lives and life experiences. The personal is understood and analysed as political through the method. It has made the intimate and the domestic sphere into object of collective inquiry, encompassing questions of the body, pleasure and sexuality, domestic violence and distribution of labour. In this, the attempt of women's economic empowerment organisations to generate change in a controlled and predicted way, to reach specific quantifiable outputs, stands in contrast with the feminist drive of the radical strands of feminism to go beyond the controlled and the predictable, to imagine the possibility of another reality and to strive for its realisation.

Today, such politicisation is beyond the objectives and capacities of all women's economic empowerment organisations I encountered, including those historically rooted in feminism. The most powerful example is that of domestic violence. In the interviews I conducted, women's economic empowerment organisations have all come in some contact with the problem of domestic violence. When domestic violence issues come up—and they inevitably come up in settings where women come together to reflect on their life—the organisations develop their own ways dealing with it, such as directing women to hotlines and services for women coping with violence and abuse. As women seriously considered leaving their husbands, some organisations came up with integration of contents designed to "strengthen the family". Practitioners tell anecdotes about high divorce rates with a sense of embarrassment I mentioned earlier, as if they were caught, like children doing something wrong. While spousal support is often perceived as a condition for women's success as entrepreneurs, and can be included in entrepreneurship training curriculums, there is no space to discuss gender and sexuality and to politicise it in a way characteristic of consciousness-raising method. There is no space to question the family institution, its relation to women's economic independence and social autonomy, and to explore these questions in depth. The setting of economic empowerment, regardless of the explicit space it provides to personal growth, entails spaces of dynamic psychological process and self-reflection for women participants. The setting does trigger a process of consciousness-raising that in its outcomes and effects transcends the original intentions of the organisers and facilitators. Simply put, the facilitators seek to empower women to become self-confident and less oppressed, but they do not—for a great deal of structural constraints—radically question the institutions of family, of heterosexuality, of subjection of women's bodies and desires, domestic violence, motherhood. In short, all the topics which were at the heart of feminist consciousness and women's critical engagement with society and economy not only in the second wave, but also in the early versions of socialist feminism since the beginning of the twentieth century and in diverse feminist trajectories around the world. This is not to idealise or romanticise the second wave, which has been extensively scrutinised for its whiteness, heteronormativity, transphobia, and overall failure to capture the radical differences and inequalities among women and their life conditions and experiences, thereby reproducing multiple systems of power and oppression. Rather, my purpose here is to highlight how feminist methods have been adopted in a way that stripped them for their explosive and disruptive potential, and that have shifted consciousness transformation from a catalyser of collective political change to a means of self-management and constitution of entrepreneurial subjectivity.

This shift can partly be explained by the contemporary institutional settings of civil society and NGO culture, structure and institutional life, which were relatively foreign to most consciousness-raising groups of the second wave and other feminist grassroots initiatives across time and space, freed from administrative and financial pressures, organising largely outside of state and market institutions. Today, in the context of economic empowerment, there are concrete goals to achieve in a limited time, from empowering women to open a certain number of microbusinesses to reporting on certain increase in income. Results need to be produced, documented, and reported to donors. Compartmentalisation is characteristic of the NGOisation process, so that some organisations focus on economic empowerment and others on domestic violence, with minimal overlap. NGOs are expected to occupy a narrowly defined niche and to professionalise in it, competing over limited resources with other NGOs. Broader social justice analysis and engagements are carried out by civil society organisations under and against these structural limitations and pressure.

To this I suggest one more explanation, one of reluctance to develop a feminist consciousness. Sandra Lee Bartky (1997), among the earlier powerful feminist voices in psychology, eloquently explained how "feminist consciousness is a consciousness of victimisation". It is a divided consciousness in that it means seeing oneself as a victim who has suffered injury at the hands of society, but also a joyous consciousness, of realising new possibilities for oneself. For Bartky, the realisation of women's oppression is not enough to constitute a feminist consciousness: it also requires apprehending women's liberation from oppression possible. Women's economic empowerment programmes offer participants a degree of self-esteem along with awareness to external factors, just enough to account for their existence and to hopefully free the participants from the weight of guilt and full responsibility for their own marginalisation. However, this degree evidently does not lead to a feminist consciousness in the sense that Bartky describes, on the contrary: empowerment focused on increasing self-esteem and self-confidence works directly against the consciousness of victimisation. These structural factors—such as discrimination in the labour market and a double burden of paid labour and domestic work—may be apprehended as wrong and unjust. Nonetheless, they are not apprehended as an occasion for active struggle of the women—certainly not within the curriculums of empowerment, although some of the practitioners may be activists on these matters outside of their work hours. Discrimination in the labour market or a double burden are criticised but are still accepted as part of reality. The aspiration is not to turn the social order of victimisation upside down, but rather to survive it a little better.

The final aspect of the entrepreneurial self is the "personal spark", as it emerges in contrast with necessity-driven entrepreneurship. Women's economic empowerment NGOs recognise that many women come to them because of restricted access to traditional employment in the labour market. This recognition of necessity-driven entrepreneurship involves a catch. Entrepreneurial endeavours, even if successful, do not change the persistent reality of structural barriers in access to employment. At the same time, this recognition may lead to stigmatisation of entrepreneurs from marginalised social groups as reluctant or not-as-good entrepreneurial subjects. This may have an effect on the quality of services, provision of credit, and other institutional interaction with entrepreneurs. In reality, research shows a complexity of push-and-pull factors leading to one's decision to become an entrepreneur. It clearly demonstrates that it is not possible to reduce complex considerations to the binary of choice versus necessity. Even members of the most marginalised and vulnerable social groups have diverse and complex considerations in choosing their path.

Consider the following excerpt from an interview with a senior employee of microfy, an Israeli NGO initially established to provide micro-credit to African refugees and asylum-seekers, in which she shared her impressions of their constituency: "For the women, they don't really have a lot of employment opportunities and they kind of see it as a way to make money. For the men [...] they often can make more money being employed, but it's more of being in control, more of a dignity thing, of being my own boss, they might be something who in their home country worked and had a degree, and here working in a hotel or cleaning, and there is very little control there, so in having a business, there's more control about that, but it's a big risk, especially without a licence, but you can see that it's a way to be in control, because also at work they can easily be fired, and here it's more stable. So there's a lot of emotional motivations, beyond financial." Once entrepreneurship is recognised as necessity-driven, it stands in tension with voluntary ethos of entrepreneurship.

Importantly, I have found that this recognition does not lead NGOs to reduce their participants and their entrepreneurial endeavours to this necessity, to stigmatise them as inferior entrepreneurs. They realise that while women's entrepreneurship may be necessity-driven, it is not all that it is. As noted before, women's economic empowerment NGOs understand micro-entrepreneurship to be a strategy to advance women's economic independence, rather than an end in itself. ISI e.V. explicitly state that in their English-language invitation to potential participants: "Less and less persons can expect to find a secure permanent job. Immigrant women have the highest rate of unemployment. Creating your own business is an alternative." Other NGOs make similar statements.

I was curious to understand the decisive factor: What makes micro-entrepreneurship a solution for some women, and not others? This direction of inquiry is made all the more important in light of the necessity-driven, even if not necessity-exclusive, nature of this entrepreneurship. If necessity is common to all women who could benefit from this path, what makes it unsuitable for some of them? I was impressed by the meeting in the Berlin office of a small microcredit provider Goldrausch e.V, established by and for women. The Coordinator hosted me for our interview in a pleasant and warm room, with a burning candle on the table. Clearly, an effort is made to make the process as supportive and least intimidating as possible for women. Nonetheless, how can a microcredit body decide whether to give a loan to a woman who has no capital and no guarantees? In Goldrausch and other microcredit providers, I inquired practitioners directly about these decisive factors. The answers often turned to individualistic notions of a woman's drive, her own determination, initiative, attitude, her "entrepreneurial spirit" and a "personal spark" in her eyes. It is something that practitioners could not express in words, but they knew it is there once they saw it: "It is this power, it is this passion [...] and there is also the question—what happens if you cannot return the loan, and then she says – I will go to work and I will pay it back. And a person feels it, you cannot describe it. And then the decision is made and then the woman gets the loan within three weeks."

Economic empowerment and entrepreneurship training assume a transformation induced by self-governance and self-control. Yet, the discourse of 'personal spark' demands to produce precisely that something very specific and authentic which is out of control. Entrepreneurial myth requests some kind of drive, passion, energy, that is almost uncontrollable and bursts out forward, innovation that defies conventionality. The programmes of empowerment are designed to bring women closer to fulfil these individualistic requirements, but the mission is difficult to say the least. Recalling the opening quote of Ilani, this mission is at odds with the workings of the social, economic and political conditions of women's lives. This personal spark, this passion, this thing one cannot describe, is clearly in tension with the structural nature of immigrant and ethnic minority women's marginalisation in the labour market and the inaccessibility of traditional employment, which is not dependent on any personal traits. Social and economic marginalisation works, after all, against one's "personal spark". It is ironic that marginalised women who are excluded from the labour market and subjected to intersectional axes of oppression, whose self-esteem is repeatedly under attack from social institutions—from the traditional family to state authorities—can be expected to project personal spark, to demonstrate some unconstrained entrepreneurial spirit. Psychological research convincingly documents how poverty, discrimination and economic inequality constitute predictors of depression in women, among the many other consequences on mental and physical health. While these structural factors working against women's personal spark can be recognised, the inability to demonstrate it can still serve as a deal breaker for the approval of microcredit.

In conclusion, the construction of the entrepreneurial self is a central and challenging task for women's economic empowerment organisations. Entrepreneurship as an institution, and entrepreneur as an ideal *homo economicus* (Tedmanson et al., 2012), are ideologically, socially and culturally marked in terms of masculinity, whiteness, youth and educated class. This marking still prevails in public imagination and in policy-making, and women from marginalised community are generally incompatible with most of these markers. One indicator of this incompatibility is the gap between women micro-entrepreneurs and the legal-administrative categories of entrepreneurship, although these are criticised even from the standpoint of young, white, educated and well-off men entrepreneurs, particularly micro-entrepreneurs and start-up owners. The outcomes of this gap differ among constituencies and among countries—some women experience persistent deviation from the norm, while other women function outside the formal economy altogether, and refrain from registering and thus from becoming an entrepreneur in a legal sense, due to the harsh economic consequences of the registration. Policy-makers increasingly acknowledge that entrepreneurship is not a gender-neutral endeavour, which leads to various top-down gender-mainstreaming initiatives. While in recent decades new modes of entrepreneurial representation gain ground, such as female entrepreneurship and immigrant entrepreneurship, they come with their own set of problems, as either flawed entrepreneurial subjects or as marked by specific class. Critical examination of one such initiative, EU's Female Entrepreneurship Ambassadors' Network, reveals its socio-economic class boundaries, evident in the absence of an intersectional approach. Gender perspective in itself does not guarantee that other social hierarchies characteristic of entrepreneurship will not reproduced. Contemporary critique of neoliberal feminism in mainstream empowerment discourses helps understand why.

Grassroots NGOs like AEEW and ISI e.V. emerge out of acute awareness to the social inequalities in the labour market and society generally and are critical of the social hierarchies informing entrepreneurship as an institution, image and practice. The gap between entrepreneurship and low-income and immigrant women is their basic assumption, as they embark on economic empowerment and entrepreneurship training. In terms of their identity politics, grassroots NGOs demonstrate not only high awareness of the structural conditions influencing women's lives, but also awareness of the differences among them. For these organisations, identity politics has meant the recognition of low-income women, immigrant women, ethnic minority women, as a specific group that is particularly marginalised in social and economic terms, and to develop programmes to advance and improve their social and economic conditions. Without identity politics—particularly in the form that recognises intersections of gender, class, race/ethnicity, socio-economic status, etc.—we are left with initiatives like EU's Female Ambassadors Network and books like *Lean In*, universalising the experiences of clearly privileged women.

NGOs extensively use terminology of self-discovery and awareness to personal resources. At the same time, they guide the participants towards what needs to be discovered, to the personal resources that are desirable for an entrepreneur. Yet, women's economic empowerment organisations and women micro-entrepreneurs themselves do not only try to "fit in" in classical narratives of entrepreneurship. Located in substantially different material conditions than the normative entrepreneur, they challenge and actively redefine what entrepreneurship is. The necessity-driven nature of their entrepreneurship serves as a vantage point to explore its difference from what is known as opportunity-driven entrepreneurship, which is essentially voluntary in spirit. More importantly, it serves to de-stabilise the binary between necessity and opportunity. The recognition of necessity does not come at the expense of recognition of women's talents, capacities and creativity—in other words, at the expense of stigmatising them as "damaged" entrepreneurs. Yet, I have pointed out a paradox in expecting individualistic notions of "entrepreneurial spirit" and "personal spark" to emerge under external conditions of necessity and economic distress that are anything but conductive to sparks and spirits.

While the entrepreneurial self or the self-enterprising individual can be seen as a prototype of neoliberal subjectivity, this subjectivity is not gender-neutral. In fact, neoliberalism constitutes marginalised women as the entrepreneurial individual and as its exception simultaneously. With empirical evidence, I strove to show how, on the one hand, marginalised women undergo training to develop and embrace the entrepreneurial way of thinking, experiencing, expressing themselves, and acting in the world. On the other hand, the field of women's economic empowerment is built upon a series of gendered assumptions and norms that outright contradict the entrepreneurial self-interested ethos. Notably, these very assumptions and norms are among the factors that make women more reliable clients and a better investment, from better repayment rates to the tendency to invest the earnings for the benefit of the family.

Finally, understanding empowerment as a technology of citizenship, I discussed that the training programmes are not invested in producing citizens with feminist consciousness. If Sandra Bartky is right and feminist consciousness requires two elements: recognition of women's disadvantaged condition and envisioning a possibility of different conditions, then the second condition is largely absent from the field of women's empowerment, and the first is compromised and attempted only to a controlled and controllable limit. What is envisioned, explicitly, is better survival under existing conditions.

References

Ahl, H., & Marlow, S. (2012). Exploring the Dynamics of Gender, Feminism and Entrepreneurship: Advancing Debate to Escape a Dead End? *Organization, 19*(5), 543–562.

Anderson, E. (2000). Beyond Homo Economicus: New Developments in Theories of Social Norms. *Philosophy & Public Affairs, 29*(2), 170–200.

Bartky, S. L. (1997). *Foucault, Femininity, and the Modernization of Patriarchal Power*. Routledge.

Bührmann, A. D. (2010). Das unternehmerische Leitbild in der Gründungsberatung. In A. Bührmann, U. L. Fischer, & G. Jasper (Eds.), *Migrantinnen Fründen Unternehmen: Empirische Analysen und Innovative Beratungskonzepte* (pp. 45–66). Rainer Hampp Verlag.

Cruikshank, B. (1999). *The Will to Empower: Democratic Citizens and Other Subjects.* Cornell University Press.

Davies, W. (2016). *The Limits of Neoliberalism: Authority, Sovereignty and the Logic of Competition.* Sage.

Gibson-Graham, J. K. (1997). The End of Capitalism (As We Knew It): A Feminist Critique of Political Economy. *Capital & Class, 21*(2), 186–188.

McRobbie, A. (2013). Feminism, the Family and the New 'Mediated' Maternalism. *New Formations, 80*(80), 119–137.

Rottenberg, C. (2014). The Rise of Neoliberal Feminism. *Cultural Studies, 28*(3), 418–437.

Sa'ar, A. (2014). Economic Empowerment of Disempowered Women: A Mediating Concept of Competing Definitions of Reality. *Theory & Criticism, 42*, 151–174. (Hebrew).

Śledzik, K. (2013). Schumpeter's View on Innovation and Entrepreneurship. In S. Hittmar (Ed.), *Management Trends in Theory and Practice.* Faculty of Management Science and Informatics, University of Zilina & Institute of Management by University of Zilina.

Tedmanson, D., Verduyn K., Essers C., & Gartner W.B. (2012). Critical Perspectives in Entrepreneurship Research. *Organization 19 (5)*: 531–541.

CHAPTER 6

Economic Empowerment, Ethno-National Citizenship

Women's economic empowerment discourses and programmes position gender, implicitly or explicitly, as the main axe of inequality. Yet, empowerment programmes take place in national and global contexts of profound and multiple forms of inequality, delineated by colonial and neo-colonial divisions, race and ethnicity, class and other forms of social stratification that are rarely spotlighted and problematised in these discourses. This is the main question of this chapter: What are we to make of economic empowerment of racialised, migrant and ethnic minority women in national and global contexts that structurally and continuously disempower them and their communities of belonging?

One of the pretences of neoliberalism is that the market largely dwells above race and class divisions, that the pursuit of profit maximisation obliterates old-fashioned prejudice, that you are judged by your professional performance. Of course, the human factor is not denied. It is recognised that individuals may and do hold prejudices or act in a discriminatory matter and so entire industries of diversity, racial sensitivity and multicultural trainings are called to treat the human factor problem, in the private and increasingly the public sectors. Yet, these are not perceived as inherent or structural problems of the market, and even more so, of entrepreneurship. On the contrary, neoliberalism positions the market as best placed to solve social, economic and even political problems of our time, with available financial resources and efficiency that the nation-state, with its

I. Michaeli, *Women's Economic Empowerment*,
https://doi.org/10.1007/978-3-030-89281-4_6

cumbersome bureaucracy and corruption, lacks. We can recognise this ideology as the backwind behind many neoliberal processes, such as the privatisation of public services, education and health. The promise of cost-efficiency and better service is made repeatedly, and it is widely believed despite its frequent record of higher costs and worse service, and despite evidence-based research, that proves the contrary.

Chapters 3 and 4 examined the institutional politics of women's economic empowerment and analysed how civil society has re-engaged with state and market actors in a neoliberal contract, reproducing the hegemony of neoclassical economics. Chapter 5 proceeded to the micro level, to comprehend which empowered and entrepreneurial citizens the field strives to produce, centring the role of gender in this process. In this chapter, I consolidate macro and micro levels of analysis of women's economic empowerment, and foreground them in their national contexts of ethnic citizenship and racialised hierarchies. I have already noted that Germany and Israel present an interesting case for comparison due to the strong ethnic dimension in their respective models of citizenship. In this chapter, citizenship regimes shift from the background to the front, focusing on the ethno-national dimension of citizenship as it materialises and operates in the field of women's economic empowerment.

Programmes of economic empowerment target primarily women of ethnic and national minorities because they are particularly marginalised in the labour market. Correlation between economic marginalisation, race and ethnicity is not unique to Israel and Germany. Among high-income countries, however, both countries score particularly high on the limitations imposed by one's ethno-national background on socio-economic mobility. I have chosen to focus economic empowerment and entrepreneurship training in organic contexts of women of diverse identities, unlimited to one ethnic, religious or national group. However, I also mentioned the considerable differences among them; indeed, national discourses take fundamentally different forms in relations to different groups, and require careful attention to specific identities. Not all racialised and ethnic minorities are equally "other" to the nation in these citizenship regimes, nor are they equally marginalised in economic terms as well. Ethnic and other minorities that are excluded from the nation, are excluded differently, have different histories, and their exclusion is differently justified, practiced and motivated. While women of various ethnic minorities may constitute a single target group for economic empowerment, how they have come to constitute this target group is a story rooted in concrete political histories and trajectories of citizenship. Furthermore, formal ethnic affiliation to the majority in an ethno-national citizenship regime may not in itself suffice to achieve belonging in the sense of membership in society, as is the case with Aussiedler and Spätaussiedler in Germany, and Mizrahi, Russian-speaking and Ethiopian Jews in Israel. In societies where belonging requires being ethnic German or Jewish, one can always be the wrong kind of ethnic German and the wrong kind of Jew.

Generally, discourses of empowerment imply that a constituency for empowerment has previously been disadvantaged by its current circumstances and its historical conditions, and deprived of social, economic, cultural or political power, capital, resources and opportunities. But how and why have they been disempowered? Examining programmes of economic empowerment and their explicit rationale, we find that disempowerment is rarely analysed and explained in detail. If empowerment is a process, disempowerment surely is a process too. Research informed by feminist theory and intersectionality has meticulously documented how migrant and minority women are continuously disempowered by ethno-national, class and gender stratification of their respective societies. Minority women experience inequality in all spheres of social life—lack of access to quality education, limited employment opportunities, unattainable public housing, and shortage of affordable childcare. When empowerment is individualistic and forward-looking, disempowerment is structural and has a long history. When we take into consideration broader historical processes that have constituted and shaped the socio-economic inequalities we encounter today, disempowerment comes to encompass more than repeated instances of workplace discrimination. It extends to histories of colonisation, ethnic cleansing, forced displacement and dispossession, annexation of land and natural resources, state policy to deny infrastructure, to name a few. Yet, these root causes of many current socio-economic inequalities are located outside the discourses of empowerment. While a comprehensive exploration of these histories is beyond scope, they nonetheless provide the necessary context for this discussion. They also make clear that the disempowered condition of a certain population cannot be assumed to be a failure of citizenship if the citizenship regime is essentially predicated on domination and dispossession of that population (Tatour, 2019).

Women of racialised, ethnic and other minorities participating in economic empowerment programmes navigate in a complex amalgam of empowering and disempowering forces and institutional practices. From this perspective, I articulate empowerment as an engagement with national histories and trajectories of citizenship (in its multi-dimensional sense) that generate, manage and sustain disempowerment of minorities along the lines of gender, ethno-national identity, and class, among other variables. Liberal and even conservative forces in civil society and governance institutions passionately advocate for labour market participation as a strategy for social inclusion of immigrants and ethnic minorities. Entrepreneurship training programmes targeting women and ethnic minorities and immigrants promise an alternative to the lack of employment opportunities, financial stability and ultimately a place in society. Yet, we shall see that when women's economic empowerment NGOs engage with economically marginalised ethnic minorities, they encounter daily the ideological and institutional structures of citizenship that produce and sustain this marginalisation, that reproduce socio-economic stratification along the lines of ethnicity and nationality. In other words, this chapter explores how the discursive and institutional structures of ethno-national citizenship operate in the field of women's economic empowerment and micro-entrepreneurship, against the backdrop of neoliberal promises of equality and belonging via market incorporation.

The definition of constituencies for economic empowerment is rooted within the specific national contexts and trajectories of citizenship. ISI e.V. in Germany defines its target audience as immigrant women, while AEEW in Israel targets low-income women, a category that is nonetheless strongly coloured in racialised and ethno-national colours. The realisation that immigration, as an experience and a structural condition, produces a specific form of marginalisation in Germany, is reflected in the ideology and practice of ISI e.V. and its slogan "for migrant women, by migrant women". The staff and the team of lecturers and facilitators come from diverse backgrounds and share first-hand migration experience. They speak of relationship of trust and comfort for migrant women who come for the entrepreneurship courses, compared to courses where only German facilitators teach. Practitioners emphasise that migrant women can expect better understanding for themselves and their situation, and even share personal problems that might have indirect connection if at all to their entrepreneurship plans.

The establishment of the organisation, as noted in Chap. 3, was initially triggered by the impact of post-reunification macroeconomic policies on immigrant women, the high unemployment rates and lack of access to professional qualification opportunities. The factor of migration remains significant for labour market participation in Germany. To begin with, imperfect command of the German language and state's unrecognition of one's professional qualification are among the main obstacles shared by immigrants. Practitioners agree that while there are many different reasons behind the decision to pursue entrepreneurship and become self-employed, the dominant reason heard in ISI e.V. is the difficulty of access to the German labour market.

One of the greatest obstacles, particularly for migrants from global South to the North, is the lack of recognition of professional qualifications and degrees. Since 2012, Germany has been introducing reforms to improve labour integration of migrants and refugees, known as the Recognition Acts. Yet, practitioners testify that these reforms have not solved the problem for the migrant women coming to programmes like ISI e.V., and overall for migrants from global South countries. The restrictions on recognition of foreign qualifications and educational certificates are publicly justified by discourses of objectivity and neutral commitment to ensure genuine and high-quality qualifications. However, as Sommer (2021) insightfully shows, the decision not to recognise foreign qualifications is a political one, and an objective assessment is simply not possible. The assessment depends on many factors, from the level of cooperation between Germany and the origin country (placing most migrants and refugees from the global South in stark disadvantage) to the present-day shortage and excess in the German labour market that influence one's chances to have their certificate recognised.

Women coming to projects like ISI e.V. experience this first-hand. When their degrees are not recognised, and re-studying their profession might take a number of years and entail costs they may not afford, self-employment becomes an alternative. Yet, even when their education is recognised, they still cannot find a job. As a practitioner put it, "It is very hard, still, for foreigners and women, to find a workplace compatible with their qualification [...] if they do hire [immigrant women], they hire women for a few hours a day, or as cheap labour, and none of those with academic education wants to go there. If they do look for people with academic education, then only Germans. So to speak, with German education and with German roots." Practitioners also point out the gap between formal equality and the prevalence of negative attitudes and stereotypes-based nationality and ethnicity in the German labour market, and that employers are taken aback by cultural difference or religion. "Although we have equality of rights, but still, if two women will come and apply for a job, one from France and the other one from Turkey, they will take the French woman." Country of origin and occupation play a big role, and so for migrants from the United States or Western Europe finding work that matches their qualifications is easier than for those coming from South America or Eastern Europe. With that said, certain occupations are stereotypically associated with particular background: “[I]nformatics specialists from Eastern Block are valued highly, so for them it is easier to find work, they don’t come to us. For the others it is quite hard.”

The articulation of immigrants as a category allows women’s economic empowerment organisations like ISI e.V. to generate recognition of the structural conditions and experiences common to immigrant women, without reducing the ethno-national differences among them. While this discourse establishes immigrants as its key category of identity, this does not serve to produce a homogenised category. Instead, it creates and sustains a certain irreducible dimension of similarities and differences. I found celebration of ethno-national diversity and heterogeneity of immigrant women to be a strong characteristic of the organisational culture. Already in the first minutes of my entrance to ISI offices, my interviewee immediately introduced to me to all the women in the hall, proudly demonstrating the international nature of the space: this one is from India, this one is from Turkey, and these two ladies here are from ex-Yugoslavia.

In this, ISI significantly differs from more limited and homogenous conceptions of immigrant women, as experienced by immigrant women in hegemonic institutional settings. State and municipal authorities regulating and offering services related to employment and self-employment, do recognise “migrants” as a category. Yet, the assumptions made about the category were problematic, and subsequently have had negative effects on the quality of service provided to women. Practitioners note that women migrants from the global South are offered jobs for which they are significantly overqualified. Consider also the first-hand experiences of a highly educated professional with migration background, describing her encounters with Germany’s Federal Employment Agency. When she started her self-employment, she was referred to coaching for people starting a business: “I didn’t feel at all that I belong there. Because I thought it’s [suited for] this woman with a small shop, or a seamstress, and my life is totally different.” Entrepreneurial support services provided by the state to women “with migration background”, as the German terminology goes, are embedded with assumptions on this target group: who they are and what their needs are. The construction of migration background as a marker of a socially and economically marginalised identity is not merely a neutral description of reality, nor is it a simple recognition in the urgent socio-economic needs of many immigrants. The perception of this category as unified rather than diverse, results in construction of immigrants as essentially, socio-economically marginalised.

Compared to ISI, its Israeli counterpart AEEW defines its target group as low-income women and women from the disadvantaged sectors of society. The avoidance of migration terminology in favour of socio-economic one is rooted in the concrete social and political significance bestowed upon the phenomenon of migration in Israel, although the local feminist discourse in which AEEW is grounded does entail recognition of ethno-national identities. In the discourse and practice of AEEW, the main visible axe of identity within the category of low-income women is ethno-national, within which migration history is incorporated: Arab-Palestinian, Mizrahi, Russian-speaking and Ethiopian women. These categories do exist in the discourse of the organisation, although in its publications, AEEW primarily refers to Jewish and Arab women. Russian-speaking and Ethiopian Jews and their families have migrated in the 1990s and 2000s, under the Law of Return which facilitates the immigration of those it recognises as Jews. Mizrahi women are often second- and third-generation immigrants, as Jews from North African and Middle Eastern countries migrated to Israel mostly in the 1950s.

The recognition of ethno-national identities is best understood against AEEW's feminist background and identity politics that developed in the feminist discourse and politics in Israel since the 1980s (Dahan-Kalev, 2001). The importance of inclusion and representation of Arab and Mizrahi women was institutionalized in the Israeli feminism in the course of the 1990s, through the 'quarters policy', a principle of equal representation for Arab-Palestinian, Mizrahi, lesbian and "other" (presumably hegemonic, Jewish Ashkenazi, heterosexual) women, with increasing attention to other marginalised identities not fitting into one of the quarters. Russian-speaking and Ethiopian immigrant women, although not part of Israeli feminist 'quarter policy', have such a massive presence on the economic margins of society, that they could not be overlooked by AEEW. In everyday talk, practitioners do pay attention to differences between the groups of women, although they acknowledge these are stereotypes. One may hear that Russian women are more ambitious and risk-taking, that Mizrahi women are more cautious about their minimal state income, or that they have been far more successful in reaching Palestinian rather than Ethiopian women. Yet, the field leaves little space to reflection on the political forces that allocate these groups substantially different positions in the Israeli society, class structure and the labour market.

As noted before, the development of Israeli feminism largely takes place within Zionist ideology and denial of Israel's historical and present injustice towards the Palestinian people (Shalhoub-Kevorkian 2012). Israeli feminists, including those on the Left, have engaged extensively with questions of inequality among women, but rarely if at all understood and questioned Israel as a settler-colonial project. Indeed, in the Israeli feminist politics of identity, Palestinian women can be acknowledged in their Arab identity to be represented alongside Mizrahi and lesbian identities. Yet, with a few exceptions, they could not expect recognition of their Palestinian identity and understanding of their economic conditions in the full political context of their oppression by the Israeli citizenship regime. Palestinian feminists in Israel have been problematising their exclusion, and the exclusion of their history and current realities, from Israeli feminism. Yet, the lion's share of their energies has been directed to autonomous organising and development of distinct Arab-Palestinian feminisms, feminist organisations and activism in gender-mixed Palestinian associations and political parties. The Mizrahi Jews, as Yali Hashash (2017) notes, are located in a complex position, belonging to economic and political margins, but also members of the Jewish hegemonic group, which entails certain opportunities for socio-economic mobility. She notes the double effect of the neoliberal transitions in Israel on the Mizrahim: those who made it in the market economy, and those who were fixed even more to the margins, in the neoliberal spirit of self-blame. While economic empowerment is a site of daily struggle with these realities and their consequences, the space for critical reflection is limited, by external factors like dependence on the state, and by internal factors of national ideologies dominating much of the Israeli civil society.

In a transnational perspective, the definition of target groups for economic empowerment reflects trajectories of citizenship particular to each national context, and the way these trajectories are interpreted by the organisations active in the field. The definition is not easily comparable. The largest minority groups in each country—German-Turkish women in Germany and Palestinian women in Israel—may face similar stereotypes and similar types of exclusion, for example as Muslim women, who can be found in both categories. Yet, in the first instance, these are women with migration history, in the second—an indigenous colonised population; and so, the ideological and political challenge each group presents to the hegemonic national identity is profoundly different. The Israeli national ethos of repatriation, or homecoming, undercuts the perception of Jewish immigrants as such, reserving the term to non-Jewish immigrants, such as migrant workers—generally referred to as foreign workers. This conceptualisation of ethnicity-based citizenship has common ideological origins and significant similarities for Germany and Israel (Weiss, 2002). In this, Israel's terms for Jewish repatriates, olim, is parallel to the German Aussiedlers, the ethnic Germans returning to Germany after decades if not centuries elsewhere. There is a notable parallel in reserving the migrant title to describe those outside the hegemonic ethnic identity or to locate them there in the first place. In the German case, the majority of immigrants in the country are mostly from the non-hegemonic ethnic group. The main category of immigrants in the Israeli case, are Jewish immigrants, those who are granted immediate citizenship upon migration, under the Law of Return.

While Muslim women are a sociological category in Germany, in the sociological discourse in Israel it is secondary to the ethno-national identification. The majority of German-Turkish women and Palestinian women in Israel are of Muslim faith, yet this is evidently more a question of Muslim women's citizenship in Germany than in Israel. The extensive literature on the Muslim women's citizenship in Germany, and specifically the labour market, concerns primarily women of Turkish origin and symbolised most strongly in the "headscarf debate". Curiously, while the most publicised struggles of Muslim women with headscarves were mainly about employment in education institutions, these debates were framed in terms of religious freedom and patriarchal oppression rather than social and economic rights, workers' rights and the right to employment. Perhaps this is because at its core, the headscarf debate is about the boundaries of the national collective and national belonging (Korteweg & Yurdakul, 2014). In contrast, although most of the Arab-Palestinian population in Israel is Muslim, their construction as a sociological category is generally as Arabs, or Palestinians when they claim their Palestinian identity, but rarely as Muslim—except when Muslim religion is invoked as an orientalist explanation for women's inferior status. The primarily othering category in the Israeli citizenship regime is racialised ethnic affiliation to Arab identity and a contrast to the Jewish identity, although it is in itself a complex and constantly contested mix of religious, cultural, ethnic and national elements in the definition of a Jew. This does not mean that Muslim women in Israel do not experience specific forms of social and economic exclusion.

Specifically in relation to the labour market, in Israel as in Germany, Muslim women report particular forms of discrimination. The most obvious example is the outspoken refusal of employers to hire a woman with a headscarf, despite the illegality of such discriminatory practice. Outside of an analytical discussion, different forms of exclusion—ethnic, national, religious, cultural—do not unfold in neatly divided categories, but merge and intertwine in their expression in everyday interactions and social life.

The root causes of disempowerment, I argued, are hardly ever explicitly discussed in women's economic empowerment programmes NGOs and programmes. Although this perceived disempowered state is the precondition for empowerment, root causes are rarely spelled out beyond general acknowledgement and statements about women, immigrants or minorities facing difficulties or being disadvantaged in the labour market. Descriptions of empowerment programmes rarely elaborate on the concrete reasons and historical origins of disempowerment, and especially on the forces, actors and institutions producing and reproducing this disempowerment. Why is this so? Are the reasons for disempowerment of women and ethnic minorities truly so self-evident and undisputable? I suggest that the opposite is true. The audiences of NGO reports on their activities, even more than potential participants, are the funders and institutional partners: from state agencies to foundations privately owned by wealthy families to banks and financing institutions. These different institutions hold different understanding of socio-economic inequalities and their root causes, and a criticism of the dominant citizenship ideologies beyond the state's comfort would likely cost NGOs their funding.

To what extent nation-states predicated on privileging one ethnic group over another, are able or willing to accommodate the empowerment of ethnic and national minorities? The answer depends, of course, on how empowerment is understood. Is it about shifting economic, social and political power, or is it about a humble increase in self-generated income and lesser reliance on welfare and public services? This question maintains its relevance even as we recall that the state is not a monolithic and coherent entity, and its authorities and institutions may have conflicting agendas. We have also seen, in Chap. 3, that civil society, state and market institutions may have different agendas and different understanding of socio-economic inequality causes and solutions, even as they all partner on one and the same programme or project. Ultimately, who and what is that citizen that the state empowers you to become, and how does that relate to your citizenship trajectory? It is very likely the citizen who relies on her own potential, who does not politically challenge the ethno-national hierarchies of the state, who embraces the promise of market opportunities over political engagement with historical injustices. As the comparative literature on citizenship asserts for countries like Germany and Israel, ethnic dimension stands in structural tension with the inclusion of ethnic minorities and their democratic and civil claims (Levy & Weiss, 2002). I am interested in understanding where women's economic empowerment, with its aspiration for inclusion and equality, stands vis-à-vis this tension. What does the neoliberal subject-position of the self-enterprising citizen means in an ethnic citizenship regime? What does it mean to be a colonial or otherwise racialised subject and a self-enterprising citizen at the same time?

Let us consider two constituencies of economic empowerment, marginalised also in comparison to other minorities in their respective countries—Turkish women in Germany and Palestinian women in Israel. While Turks are historically immigrants in Germany, and Palestinians are an indigenous population and part of a people struggling for national liberation, these largest minorities in these respective countries are politically, socially and economically marginalised. These are, essentially, two different forms of exclusion in ethnic citizenship regimes. Adding a gender layer, the respective participation rates of Turkish and Palestinian women in the labour market are significantly lower in relation to the general population, to women of other ethnic minorities, and to the men in their own communities.

Women's economic empowerment programmes, particularly in official state discourses but also in civil society discourses, are constructed as an alternative form of labour market integration for women, immigrants and ethnic minorities. However, while the state nominally supports for the employment of women from ethnic and national minority groups, this hegemonic discourse persistently shifts the responsibility for high unemployment rates towards the women themselves, their families and their communities. This is true for Germany as it is for Israel. A recurring reason quoted in this debate is the concept of tradition, framing Arab, Turkish and Muslim religious and cultural traditions as the decisive factor that prevents women's participation in the labour market. In a public conference in 2009, the Israeli Finance Minister Yuval Steinitz addressed Palestinian women's unemployment to "cultural obstacles" and "traditional frameworks" allegedly characteristic to Arab societies. This statement is not exceptional but rather exemplary of a particular common sense throughout official discourses. In fact, culture and tradition cannot fully explain the low participation of Arab women in the Israeli workforce, also in comparison with Arab women's employment in other countries (Zoabi, 2009). In Israel, a range of structural and institutional factors undermines the employment and labour market access for Arab-Palestinian women. The frequent repetition of the tradition factor by policy-makers contributes to its cultivation as a form of common sense. The popularity of this explanation is astonishing, given that traditional and patriarchal family and community structures are but one of several factors restricting women's access to the labour market. While this discourse manifests in the specific field of women's economic empowerment in Germany and Israel, it is recognisant of far broader and global orientalist discourses about non-Western women. This rhetorical tendency has major implications for policy-making. Shifting the responsibility for economic inequality towards women and their communities obscures from view and from policy-making the structural obstacles that the state not only allows, but also, as we shall see, actively sustains.

Rottmann and Marx Frerree (2008) find that many prominent German feminists share the hegemonic perspective, which sees Muslim women oppressed as women (by Muslim men), while failing to see the oppression they face from the state as members of Muslim or Turkish communities in Germany. From this perspective, the German state is expected to liberate women from the former, while de facto allowing—if not actively immersing in—the latter. This perspective and the approach underlying it are non-intersectional, in that they fail to capture the multiple social relations and modalities that shape the lives of marginalised women. The authors conclude that social policy debates are essentially debates about state boundaries and citizenship, about "whether and when the state can be trusted to act on its citizens' behalf" (p. 501). Indeed, the discourse that shifts the responsibility on colonised and racialised women requires us to make transparent the role of the state in economic as well as social, cultural and political exclusion and violence. The tradition-centred rhetoric does not only shift the responsibility away from the state. It also positions the state as a liberating force from the patriarchal oppression, discursively constructed inherent to Arab-Palestinian, Turkish and Muslim cultures and communities. It is appropriate to recall the famous phrase used by Gayatri Spivak (1994) to describe relations in a colonial social order: "white men saving brown women from brown men". This representation of non-European and particularly Muslim women's oppression has a long history in the West. It also has a historical function in justifying and legitimising forms of colonial and imperial violence as liberation of women. Post-colonial feminist scholars have long cautioned that hegemonic interventions for gender equality, particularly the ones targeting minority women, may strengthen the stigmatisation of the communities the women belong to, and contribute to the portrayal of their cultures and communities as fixed and backward. Such broad stigmatisation ultimately fails to account for the specificities of women's oppression across contexts and to respond to them.

If shifting the responsibility is one scenario, another is to overlook the structural factors of exclusion and to focus on the motivation of the individual woman to overcome personal and social obstacles. Consider the example of the Deutsche Islam Konferenz—German Islam Conference—a platform initiated by the German government for dialogue with Muslim and Turkish communities living in the country. The 2012 Conference focused on the employment of Muslim women as one of its key themes. Conference materials draw a largely unproblematic picture of the German labour market, which contradicts empirical research on the difficulties that Muslim women face. Its publication highlights individual success stories of Muslim women—in particular Muslim women wearing headscarves—who have not encountered any problems in the labour market. Representation of success stories can undoubtedly be empowering for women and girls; however, it also risks in downplaying the significance of the external, structural factors. This representation may avoid stigmatisation of Muslim women and Muslim communities, but it also avoids social responsibility to identify and deconstruct structural obstacles embedded across social institutions, in the family and the community, but also in the labour market and the state. In the neoliberal spirit, the Muslim woman is represented as one who can overcome these obstacles through sheer will and determination, obscuring structural problems of legislation, policy, institutional and everyday racism and sexism, discrimination in access to education and employment opportunities and so on.

The rudimentary nature of both the tradition-centred explanation and the unproblematic picture of the labour market becomes all the more disturbing upon a closer look at the realities of the labour market, and the powerful and complex institutional structures that perpetuate inequalities and disadvantage Arab-Palestinian and German-Turkish women. To this end, I suggest that misrecognition—either intentional or naïve—of the root causes for labour market exclusion (i.e., disempowerment) results in failure to develop appropriate strategies for inclusion (i.e., empowerment).

The high rates of economic distress among the Palestinians in Israel have their historical roots in the British colonisation of Palestine and subsequent Israeli colonisation and formation of a Palestinian working class (Abdo, 1992). Today, for Palestinian women in Israel, the steady increase in the level of education is not sufficiently reflected in the low participation rates in the labour market and the high rates of unemployment. Moreover, the improvement in women's employment over the recent decade did not encompass all women: while it raised for young and educated, it dropped for older and uneducated women. It should also be noted that economic participation and employment status is not limited to the mere fact of one's employment, but also extends to the nature of this employment. In Israel, educated Palestinians are less likely to find employment that fits their education level. Furthermore, nearly 50% of Palestinian women are employed in low-paid and traditionally "feminine" sectors of education, personal services and health services. Diversification of occupation is essential for improvement in women's employment status (Shihadeh & Moadi, 2011). Palestinian women who are part of the labour force are primarily employed in the local market, and lack access to the central and predominantly Jewish labour market. Sociocultural and political factors both play a role, such as traditional family norms for some women, burden of reproductive labour and caretaking responsibilities, discrimination and racism in the largely Jewish labour market, and, significantly, state policies in multiple areas of life, from education to transportation. These conditions also influence women's own preferences: many women may prefer working close to home due to caretaking obligations, or distancing themselves from the central labour market to avoid a potentially hostile and racist work environment. On state policy level, the most immediate and evident obstacle is the absence of adequate public transport to Palestinian towns and villages in Israel. The problem of transport is an expression of a broader state policy of neglect of Palestinian residential areas; and, it has been on the agenda of Palestinian feminist organisations like Kayan who have identified it as a core obstacle to women's employment. Women's economic empowerment practitioners also point out to the absence of industrial areas and workplaces in the vicinity of Palestinian towns, a problem that pushes women to accept exploitative working conditions, as long as organised transportation from their hometowns is provided.

KIEDF's microcredit programme for Bedouin women in Israel presents a particularly stark example of the pitfalls of economic empowerment in realities of structural disempowerment. The microcredit programme SAWA targets Bedouin women in the south of Israel. The programme is financed by the Israeli Ministry of Economy, a fact that could have deterred women from accepting it were it made known to them. In a media interview, a ministry employee testified that the success of the programme owes to the confidentiality about the government's process, and that they are interested in keeping it this way, due to the barriers the community has towards government engagement. This narrative about SAWA perfectly illustrates the state as the saviour of Bedouin women, advancing their economic situation while humble enough to stay under the radar. In fact, critical information is deliberately withheld from Bedouin women, effectively—and deliberately—undermining their political agency. This is portrayed as a noble gesture of selflessness and generosity, rather than a political manipulation that marginalises Bedouin women even further along the lines of gender, ethnicity and nationality. Ultimately, the political agency of Bedouin women is presented as an obstacle, rather a condition, to social change. The narrative of the abovementioned media interview speaks about "deep, persistent taboos over accepting Jewish money" and addresses it to cultural pride resistance to assimilation. Women's potential refusal to take credit from the state is portrayed as false consciousness, as prejudice, and as cultural pride, a concept that sounds almost endearing in its backwards way. These notions reproduce a clearly Orientalist approach to the Bedouin community. Furthermore, terms like cultural pride de-politicise this refusal, and expressions like "taboo over accepting Jewish money" unambiguously imply charge of anti-Semitism and primordial racism. These discursive elements come together to lend further legitimacy to the act of undercutting women's political agency. There is no possibility that Bedouin women might refuse to accept credit from the state as a political act of protest against decades of state violence, discrimination, displacement and denial of the most basic services—de facto denial of their citizenship rights. There is no recognition of their right to say no, to refuse to take credit from the state, as a political act. This narrative effectively omits the political nature of relationship among Bedouin women and the state.

The erasure of Bedouin women's political agency and voice is not unique to the microcredit case. It is endemic to Israeli policies and practices in the Negev prior and since the establishment of the Israeli state, and so it is vital to account for the economic political economy which women have to navigate (Shalhoub-Kevorkian, 2012, Shalhoub-Kevorkian et al., 2014). Demolitions of homes and entire villages are but one example to the extreme violence regularly perpetrated by the state against Bedouin communities, with detrimental and gender-specific effects on Bedouin women. In unrecognised villages, Bedouin women are denied the most basic rights by the state. Nadera Shalhoub-Kevorkian (2012) focuses her discussion on human rights activism and projects that operate within colonial legal and social order, and questions their capacity to achieve rights and justice. Serving the local community in a feminist manner, she argues, requires "prioritizing women's political, civil, social and economic voices and rights, while challenging the colonial structure".

Microcredit programmes like KIEDF explain the marginalisation of Bedouin women as primarily if not exclusively a problem of patriarchy, while making state violence invisible and ignoring the historical injustice it has been inflicting on women and their communities. Asked whether there is a social mobility in microfinance, my interview partner admitted that social and economic mobility is limited for Bedouin women in Israel. Her reasoning first focused exclusively on patriarchy, yet then she added, "social mobility in Israel is many times not related to the economy. It is not related to the economic situation. A woman born Bedouin will die Bedouin. Full stop. An Ultra-Orthodox woman will always be an ultra-Orthodox woman, and she will always have that patriarch to tell her what to do [...] in Israel, all this issue of social mobility is... it is so built on things that are not... that are not the economy." In institutionalised programmes, surely those funded by the state, there is no challenge or recognition of state violence; the mere allusion to colonialism, historical or present, would be perceived as science fiction at best. Shalhoub-Kevorkian identifies similar dynamics for human rights organisations that lead interventions in the Bedouin society while disregarding the historical political context. The failure to grasp the importance of historical injustices for the community creates a gap between human rights organisations and the Bedouin women they seek or claim to serve. Similarly, economic empowerment and microcredit programmes like KIEDF operate entirely within transparent colonial logic, structure, discourse and paradigm, without, at any point, challenging ethnic citizenship ideology and institutions that strip Bedouin citizens of citizenship, un-recognise them, and effectively produce and sustain economic, as well as social and political, exclusion and marginalisation.

In the German case, a historical perspective similarly holds the explanatory power to distort hegemonic narratives, and its absence serves to reinforce paradigms of ethnic citizenship as natural and transparent. A zoom out of tradition-centred explanations reveals a complexity of historical and socio-economic factors explaining the marginalisation of German-Turkish women in the labour market. The very early tracking in schools—as early as the fourth grade—builds on social capital of the family more than anything else. While public discourse alludes to differences in the social capital of the families, and to traditional gender norms transmitted from the first generation limiting women's participation in the labour market, it obscures the level to which patriarchal order is a historical product in Germany. Labour migration from Turkey—including women's migration—dates to the 1960s. Women were recruited for unskilled labour in physically demanding jobs and industries of fishing and food processing, textile, clothing and electronics, as well as service and cleaning. In female sectors, wages were 30–40% lower than men's, so that the gender inequality in the labour market was the resultant of the West German recruitment policy. A combination of German state policies left many Turkish women without working permits, restricted them to marriage or illegal migration, and increased informal employment in domestic service—altogether leading to increased dependency on the male breadwinner. In other words, the patriarchal structure in the Turkish community is not simply an imported phenomenon, but has been strengthened and intensified by German state policies as well.

To summarise so far, women of ethnic and national minorities, colonised people or immigrants, may experience disempowerment on many levels: the family, the community, the majority society and the state. However, dominant discourses of labour market inclusion, case in point economic empowerment and microcredit, tend to focus on the former rather than the latter levels. In particular, the role of the state in disempowerment and marginalisation of racialised and colonised women is made invisible; it is effectively outside the discourse. In this way, women's economic empowerment takes place in a limited paradigm, aligned with ideological and institutional structures of ethno-national citizenship and, in Israeli case, colonial regime. Key mechanism that creates and sustains this paradigm is the erasure of historical injustices and reasons capable of explaining why and how migrant and indigenous women have come to necessitate any kind of economic empowerment in the first place.

In the final part of this discussion, let us examine some of the ways in which racialised, ethnic and national structures emerge in the practice of entrepreneurship itself. Models of micro-entrepreneurship and micro-credit common in economic empowerment programmes are predicated upon the capital of the participants, or the clients. Programmes offer various combinations of knowledge, skills and personal psychodynamic transformative processes, as Chap. 5 details. A business idea is generally not a pre-requisite to participate in economic empowerment and entrepreneurship-training programmes; it is assumed to come in the process. However, the micro-enterprise itself—the goods, the skills or the knowledge that are to be transmitted into marketable products—is assumed to be either present or easily available. The starting point of the woman entrepreneur, the economic, social and cultural capital at her disposal, is therefore critical. It is easy to see how social stratification, for example, lack of access to quality education or professional qualification, is reproduced already in this initial stage of entrepreneurship. In societies characterised by strong correlation of class and race/ethnicity, this means that women from racialised and ethnic minorities are disadvantaged already in their starting point.

When it comes to this starting point, the heterogeneity among minorities and immigrants is significant. A highly educated immigrant woman, whose professional qualification is not recognised in Germany, may still possess a relatively high degree of social and cultural capital—networks of support and personal connections, skills and knowledge that can still be converted into marketable products, and the social recognition and legitimacy granted to her by the potential clientele. Women with unrecognised education and professional background in medical and health professions often open businesses in spheres such as nutrition consulting and alternative medicine. In contrast, a woman from a rural area, with elementary education and without any record of employment outside her home, can most likely build on the knowledge and skills she accumulated in household labour and in the course of recreational or social activities. Her most apparent business possibilities may include catering, cleaning, traditional or modern handcraft, retail, sales and small-scale marketing. Women without higher education (at all, or one that is officially recognised) often concentrate in so-called pink-collar jobs associated with traditional femininity: beauty and cosmetics, hairdressing, clothing retail. Femininity as a form of capital thus intersects with hierarchies of ethnicity and class (Black, 2006).

Certain ethnic groups come to be associated with low-income occupations so much that this association is widely seen as natural and ahistorical, as the following incident in an Israeli social network from 2015 illustrates. A middle-upper class Ashkenazi woman announced a social enterprise of cleaning and home maintenance services, claiming it as a form of women's economic and personal empowerment. She invited women with natural love for cleaning, residing in the neighbouring disadvantaged and primarily Mizrahi towns to work in private homes in her own town. Mizrahi feminists and their allies reacted with outrage to the implication that Mizrahi women would clean the homes of wealthier Ashkenazi women because of any natural cleaning talents and heart inclinations, and not because of institutionalised oppression of Mizrahi women. The rhetoric of "empowerment" in a project oblivious to past and present of social and economic injustice was met with a good deal of sarcasm. This example is not representative of the field of women's economic empowerment, certainly not the grassroots levels that tend to grow out of acute awareness to social and economic injustice and marginalisation of minority women. Nonetheless, it does bring to the surface the limited occupational opportunities of women in societies with strong ethno-national stratification, where race, ethnicity and nationality strongly correlate with class. Moreover, it indicates the social normalisation and naturalisation of this stratification: the concentration of a certain ethnic group in low-status and low-income occupations can seem ahistorical, natural and unproblematic to segments of the public and to policy-makers alike.

Creativity and innovation are critical in developing business ideas out of limited resources. In response to my question what do women in retail sell, one practitioner shared her experience, admitting that she herself was impressed with the possibilities that women uncover: "Everything. Yesterday there was a Russian woman [for consulting], she sells books. And sells them very well. She started with bags [...] there's for example all the women who are Mode-bewusst (fashion-minded) and they think they can sell it, there's also very narrow specialisations, for example recently we wrote a business-plan, Kleidung für Veganer (clothing for vegans). I did not even know that, I knew there's this food, but that you can also have vegan clothing". Women's economic empowerment programmes strive to train women how to capitalise on the skills, knowledge and talents that they already have. However, economic inequality and marginalisation cannot be reduced to the capacity to capitalise on the existing resources. The inequality is manifested, first and foremost, in the existing resources, and even more so in the resources one does not have, or has been deprived of her entire life. After all, the mere awareness to the existence of vegan clothing is not self-evident, and can depend on one's social and cultural capital.

The significance of the starting capital might help us understand the vast gaps identified by practitioners in Israel among different ethnic groups of women. They testify that within the target group of Jewish women, they have not been successful in working with Ethiopian women, while Russian women demonstrated more ambition, and Mizrahi women preferred to safeguard their minimal income rather than taking risks. This assessment is really the socio-economic stratification of the Israeli society reproduced in the field of women's economic empowerment: The efforts to enterprise entrepreneurial subjects produce different effects in different ethnic groups. The difficulty of this organisation to work with Ethiopian women is indeed symptomatic of the Israeli civil society. Other explanatory factors can come in force, primarily the combination between lower starting capital, education levels, and lack of tradition of self-employment and entrepreneurship in the Ethiopian community, also compared to immigrants from FSU countries. (Offer, 2004: 45). In contrast, Russian-speaking immigrant women in Israel, on average more educated and with professional qualifications more applicable to the Israeli market, are clearly in another starting position. Furthermore, immigration is a time of inevitable change and adaptation to life in new settings. Early research on the gender aspects of Russian immigration to Israel has found that despite downward socio-occupation mobility, women are better at developing strategies of adaptation (Remennick, 1999). Downward socio-occupational mobility of immigrant adults is substantially different from socio-economic marginalisation of second and third generation to immigration, such as for Mizrahi women. This difference is not just in terms of external conditions but also one's psychosocial state of being (part of Bourdieu's cultural capital), which might account for what the practitioner calls "approach", or "attitude" in rather individualistic terms.

Indeed, the obstacles to economic empowerment identified by practitioners are not only those imposed by external conditions, state policies, community or family pressure; practitioners point to the reluctance of marginalised women themselves to take drastic steps in order to transform their lives and improve their economic situation. To this end, consider the example of Mizrahi women dependent on state welfare. Practitioners note that Mizrahi women often avoid pursuing significant business growth;

taking the chance to increase their income means also risking losing welfare money, their primary economic survival strategy. This sets the desirable profit bar extremely low, and thus challenges the practitioners of economic empowerment. The problematisation of dependence on state welfare as an obstacle for women's micro-enterprise came up particularly strong in Israel, compared to Germany. This can be explained by the legal-administrative differences among the countries. In Israel, micro-business registration is quickly followed by losing one's entitlement to state welfare, referred in Israel as "guaranteed minimal income". In contrast, registering as self-employed in Germany does not entail a risk of losing state welfare altogether. The period of grace extended to the business to start generating income and profit is up to three years (in relation to the 6 months in Israel), and even as this period runs out, there are still possibilities to receive complementary income from the state. These conditions are less favourable in Israel, and thus the risk to lose one's basic income is more material. Thus, women dependent on welfare may give up in advance on the effort to generate significant income and avoiding registering their micro-enterprise, in order not to lose the guaranteed minimal income. For practitioners it constitutes a real obstacle: "I understand that, a person needs money to go to the grocery store, but that woman, if she doesn't break through, if she is dependent on the guaranteed minimal income, she will never break through. How do you do this transition? I haven't seen the trick of trade yet. I haven't found this trick."

Economic marginalisation and dependence on state welfare emerge as a kind of trap, a condition that women find hard to escape, despite their vast personal resources and experience of survival in difficult conditions. The efforts of personal empowerment and construction of entrepreneurial subjectivity, which relies on oneself rather than on the state—appear to run across a brick ceiling, when it comes to risking the guaranteed minimal income. A practitioner shared her frustration: "[A] woman with two children on a minimal income, she receives 2,600 shekels [per month]. Can you explain to me, how does she live? No Minister of Finance, no Professor of Economics would manage that. You do manage that. So take all your powers of how you manage that, and transfer it to be in a place where you make ends meet by yourself, and be the most amazing thing in the world. But we don't manage to do that." This reliance of Mizrahi women—particularly Mizrahi single mothers—on welfare has recently been analysed in depth by the anthropologist Smadar Lavie. She points to the trap of bureaucracy, defining it as "bureaucratic torture", and challenges the rational conception of bureaucracy. Instead, Lavie (2018) comprehends it as ritualistic, as "a divine cosmological order" that constructs its rituals along the lines of race, gender and religion. Lavie's rigorous ethnographic work and conclusions help us understand that women's economic empowerment organisations "don't manage to do that" for a reason. Women's refusal, reluctance or simple inability to transmit their competences of survival to the entrepreneurial field, and to break the cycle of dependence on welfare, is actively produced and reproduced by bureaucratic structures of the state. This is precisely the tension of empowerment efforts that run against a continuous process of disempowerment. Here, this tension structurally limits the potential of empowerment programmes to serve as a path of social and economic mobility. The decision not to register one's business for the fear of losing the guaranteed minimal income, substantially limits its growth and development. Among other effects, it takes away women's entitlement to a second loan with microcredit providers, and prevents them from working with established clients.

For a German example of the empowerment and disempowerment paradox, consider the case of Marie e.V. This association was established to support the women in East Germany, who were threatened with unemployment following the economic restructuring after the collapse of the German Democratic Republic and the reunification of Germany in 1989/1990. Marie e.V., like many women's empowerment organisations in Germany, is funded by the municipal authorities and the European Social Funds. Among its services, it offers trainings to women on coping with the state employment agencies. The need for this training is evident, because German employment agencies have been extensively criticised for oppressive conduct and stigmatisation of the unemployed and people living in poverty. Like many bureaucratic systems, it is famous for its arbitrariness—your fate often depends on the good will of the clerk handling your case. Although this is an experience shared widely by people in poverty, including ethnic Germans, a particularly discriminatory treatment is experienced by migrants and racialised and ethnic minorities. The state thus funds activities to train people how to cope with fear and humiliation that its own agencies generate, empowering women to manage the disempowerment they encounter in state institutions.

As ethno-national structures of citizenship reproduce inequalities in the field of women's economic empowerment, ethnic and national identity can become one of the few sources of capital for minorities. Depending on one's social and cultural capital, this can be mastering of the language and occupation in translation and inter-cultural communications and management, traditional arts and crafts, import of gastronomic, textile or cultural products from the country of origin, and so on. Fair trade and traditional handcraft are a popular focus in women's economic empowerment. Women mastering traditional handicrafts can transmit their cultural capital—knowledge and skills—into economic capital. This transition is achieved by shifting the capital across fields, from the traditional community to the free market, which is hungry for so-called authentic products. One example is Lakiya Negev Weaving Project, which engages Bedouin women in the South of Israel in producing traditional handicrafts and selling them in markets outside the Bedouin community, where the products are valued and marketed as "authentic" and "ethnic". Another example Fair Trade project of Achoti ("my sister" in Hebrew), an organisation established by Mizrahi feminists and working to advance disadvantaged women in Israel, markets products made by marginalised women from diverse backgrounds, through its central store in the centre of Tel Aviv and in additional selling points. In the store one can find, for example, clay pots for cooking made by women from Ethiopia in traditional Ethiopian hand technique, and traditional Palestinian embroidery applied to smartphone covers or bags designed for yoga mattresses, commercialising cultural hybrids of tradition and modernity. The product description tag reads: "[B]ag for a yoga mattress, decorated in Palestinian embroidery, the Tatriz, embroided with one stich, the colors and patterns are very diverse. The embroidery has an important role in representing the geographical belonging of the woman or the man wearing it. Every Palestinian city has its own unique embroidery pattern." We are reminded that commercialisation and consumption of culture and so-called authenticity has a long colonial and orientalist history. It is a strategy of economic survival, which highlights the absence of other forms of starting capital. Meanwhile, political questions of cultural appropriation of "ethnic" products counter the transparency of the consumer's whiteness and other forms of racial and class privilege. With all its promises of meritocracy, entrepreneurship is a sphere where capital is reproduced and only slowly accumulated, if at all. This can explain why different spheres of women's entrepreneurship create the feel of different worlds. In micro-entrepreneurship, women can capitalise on household and handcraft skills to manage their poverty a bit better. In entrepreneurial spheres like the Female Entrepreneurship Ambassadors Network, middle- and upper-class women can capitalise on prestigious education, professional qualification, and a range of economic, social and cultural capital.

In neoliberal discourses of gender equality that do not go as far as to question market economies, access to finance is recognised as the core problem. Financing is a profoundly gendered sphere. Intersecting with factors of race, ethnicity, class, sexuality and more, it is particularly limited for low-income and marginalised women. The assumption is that equal access would eliminate gender bias, obscuring the many ways in which financing is structured to privilege personal and social arrangements associated with traditional masculine gender roles.

Beyond own capital, women may experience inequality in access to finance and resources on three major levels: the family, the community and the financial institutions (banks and microcredit providers). On the family level, practitioners report that that married women encounter the expectations from the husband to look for their own funding, rather than tapping into the business or the family budget for an investment that may not succeed. Tension in the family is a frequent scenario. Beyond blocking access to family resources, family can serve an obstacle on other levels as well. A practitioner noted that it is not uncommon for women to be in a financially critical situation because of the husband. When men register their business on the wife's name and reach bankruptcy, the woman is not able to receive a loan for her own business—even in the case of divorce. In the case of a bad financial situation of the married couple (either or both spouses), the bank path is not an option. On the other hand, women sometimes register their business on the name of the husband. This produces a different set of problems. A practitioner spoke of a woman whose husband runs her accounts, so that she does not know how much she earns. Not because he withholds the information from her, in this particular case, but because she feels it is beyond her comprehension.

Community level encompasses formal and informal networks of support. Community networks are a valuable source of capital for men who seek to become self-employed and try opening a business. For women, the level of the community becomes especially important if they are in process of separation or divorce, and women raising children, who cannot rely on the support of their partner. Yet, at the same time, communities based on family and marriage may present extra difficulties to women who violate gender norms of proper behaviour, unmarried, separated or divorced women. When there is no access to community resources, the next step is financial institutions. A KIEDF representative explained that they have much more success working with Arab women rather than the ultra-Orthodox community, because the ultra-Orthodox community has much more resources of their own. Governmental funding enabled KIEDF to expand their work with Palestinian women in Israel. When asked about the state's motivation, the practitioner explained: "the policy is to get to a situation when populations in the country that officially don't work, enter the labour market, either by finding a job as employees or by opening a microbusiness".

Finally, the level of financial institutions. Gender bias in women's access to finance and financial institutions is well documented. For instance, banks' reluctance to work with micro-loans impacts especially women, because women tend to take smaller loans. Similarly, a business based at home tends to look less serious and professional for bank clerks and therefore be denied a loan. Here too, women tend to start and operate their business from home, in order to save unnecessary expenses but also if they are primary caretakers for children, elderly or disabled family members. This is a global problem acknowledged across national contexts. Nonetheless, a small-scale external evaluation conducted by an external evaluator for AEEW, showed that after 5 years of operating business, women tended to turn more to banks (after one year of business operation, 79.1% used self-capital and 4% requested a bank loan; after five years, 60.6% used self-capital and 13.6% requested a loan from the bank). It remains unclear whether this is due to growth in the needs of the business, women's exposure to possibilities, or a process of empowerment that prepared them to cope with the financial institutions.

Group loans is another microfinance model offered to women extensively in the global South, but also in some cases in the North. In this model, women are each other's guaranty: if one of the group members does not pay back, the others have to cash in. This model has been harshly criticised for causing breakage in communities, for generating extreme peer pressure and conflicts. While it is effective for microfinance providers in generating paybacks, it can also destroy social fabric and solidarity in marginalised communities. The very social fabric and solidarity that is so essential in organising against state policies and institutional oppression. This has far-reaching social and political consequences. Unsurprisingly, this is the model applied to the Bedouin and other Arab-Palestinian communities in Israel, and is successful from the microcredit providers' perspective, but no research has been done on the social and political consequences and costs for the community. Further knowledge on this would enable both practitioners and credit recipients to receive informed decisions.

Micro-entrepreneurship and microfinance enjoy the image of generating wealth for marginalised individuals and communities out of minor investment that returns to the investors. Despite its fair share of growing criticism, it still enjoys the popular perception of being "the magic bullet". However, actual examination of women's economic empowerment and entrepreneurship-training programmes reveals the reproduction and slow (if at all) and difficult accumulation of capital rather than the magic of social and economic mobility. To illustrate, consider the actual expenditure of microcredit loans. The funds can be used to increase qualification, purchase equipment or rent a space. For example, a cosmetician who wanted to include laser hair removal in her list of services used it to complete a qualification course and buy the laser equipment; a saleswoman selling clothes door-to-door used it to buy a car; a seamstress who already has a clientele from her ethnic community, used it to rent an atelier. Rarely but still possible under some conditions, women can use the money for studies, such as a basic English-language course for a shop owner to better communicate with tourists. However, microcredit is not a scholarship, and cannot be used to acquire secondary or higher education. A participant may complete a marketing course of one or two months—but she cannot enrol and complete an academic degree in business administration. Nonetheless, it is important to acknowledge that empowerment processes can serve as a catalyst for women to enlist for studies. In AEEW's external evaluation, studies are one of the indicators for personal empowerment, and indeed, it was found that the programme has a strong positive effect on women's decision to pursue studies. Hence, while micro-entrepreneurship and microfinance largely entail reproduction of economic, social and cultural capital along gender, racial and ethnic stratification lines, its possibilities for upwards mobility, as limited as they are, do present a value in absence of accessible alternatives.

Having discussed access to starting capital and finance, let us turn to access to markets. An entrepreneur with a starting capital and secured financing still needs a market. Self-employment and micro-entrepreneurship is a valuable option for women in societies where opportunities for employment are limited or non-existent. In some national economies, entrepreneurship is the norm—to illustrate, in India 70% of the population are self-employed. However, in countries where employment is the norm, the demand for micro-entrepreneurship service is higher in areas where it is difficult to find employment. For example, in the more remote villages and towns. In other words, a necessity-driven entrepreneurship. Paradoxically, where there is limited employment, there is likely a limited market. It is limited in terms of the size of the population, especially if the area is not well connected to the rest of the world. It is limited in terms of products this population might be interested in and may afford to consume. It is limited in terms of competition—for example, traditional crafts of Lakiya Weaving Project need to be marketed outside the community, which is enabled by the Visitor's Centre. This closed market limits occupational possibilities, goods and services that can be sold. Given the limited pool of knowledge and skills that women can capitalise on, the market easily becomes overflowing. A practitioner tells: "[L]isten, most of the Arab women I know, in our groups, come from the villages, and there, there is really more complication, because the market is different. It is family-based, and also what exactly would she do, it is not as if she... can do catering, what, they will buy food from her? Everyone cooks there. So then suddenly everyone becomes hairdressers, and everyone go and do mini-marketing and so. But... this is difficult. It is difficult to be in these places and to develop those things."

Access to market is further hindered by mass consumption patterns that privilege larger businesses and corporations over small-scale business providers. A practitioner reflected on the limitation in focusing on women micro-entrepreneurs while dealing with clientele that is disinterested in micro-enterprises. "So somehow [the public] avoids the micro businesses and go the shopping centre where you have everything. You have the hair salon, and shopping and clothing and a coffee shop and all. 'So why should I go to that woman?' and this is one of the problems, there is no real commitment here, ours too, that we cannot engage the public in this. When we are interviewed [...] the emphasis is more on – come to our courses, it's worth it, ta-ta-ta, and we don't come and say—go and buy from this woman. This is the most important thing. To open more businesses is one story, but they will not open if there will be no [buyers] to work with." We thus see how the marginalisation of women entrepreneurs is reproduced in all these spheres: starting capital, access to financing, and access to markets.

In conclusion, in this chapter I have set to consolidate macro and micro analyses of women's economic empowerment to foreground them in their national contexts of ethnic citizenship. I asked, how does economic empowerment of racialised, migrant and indigenous women operate in national contexts complicit in their structural and continuous disempowerment, and political regimes predicated on their dispossession and erasure? Taken together, empowerment and disempowerment constitute a complex amalgam of forces and processes that women navigate. Women's economic empowerment programmes are embedded in ethno-national citizenship regimes, and their very existence is a direct response to the high correlation among economic marginalisation, race and ethnicity and gender in these countries. Their target groups are constituted by this very correlation. Yet, why these groups are disempowered, how they have come to constitute a group for economic empowerment remains beyond most empowerment discourses. The disempowerment of racialised, migrant and ethnic minority women is more often than not taken as an ahistorical point of departure.

Within the allegedly meritocratic entrepreneurship sphere, gender, racial and class-based forces of exclusion continue operating on the levels of the family, community, society and the state. Most empowerment discourses tend to focus on the former, on concepts of culture and tradition, ignoring the latter. The role of the state in the continuous disempowerment of women from non-hegemonic communities is made transparent. The Israeli example of Bedouin women demonstrates how the denial of fundamental citizenship rights is not recognised as relevant to women's lives, and their economic marginalisation. The subordination of women and undercutting of their political agency is transmitted into and justified by discourses of empowerment and inclusion, "for their own good". The German example of Turkish women has also shown that while tradition and patriarchy are presented as a Turkish import, they have been strengthened by West German policies of labour market restructuring. This reinforced patriarchy is part of their German citizenship, too.

As much as the historical dimension holds an explanatory power, its dismissal serves to construct racial and ethnic others, the migrant and the colonised, as inherently disempowered, as a natural condition, with the role of the state and politics of the citizenship regime completely transparent. In the context of women's empowerment, it allows the state to position itself as the saviour of women from the shackles of tradition and patriarchy, even as the state's own policies and practices may harm women as members of oppressed racialised ethnic group and may enhance patriarchy in their communities.

While the neoliberal ethos of entrepreneurship is presented as a magic bullet, as a chance to escape the inequalities of the labour market, I have discussed some of the forms in which inequalities experienced by minorities are not avoided, but in fact reproduced, in the very practice of entrepreneuring. This reproduction of racial hierarchies of citizenship regimes is consistent with the reproduction of gender inequalities. Women's subjection in both private and public sphere—as women and as members of ethnic minorities—is touched on slightly, just enough to generate the process of improving one's self-esteem. In both outward looking aspects and in the training process itself, the responsibility is shifted on the subject, of both integration in the labour market and of family–work balance. Empowerment processes do touch on structural inequalities, but they are touched in a way designed to keep it under control, stopping short of questioning citizenship ideologies or mobilising for structural change. In previous chapters we have seen this containment operating both on the macro level of civil society and on the micro level of the subject.

Ultimately, a narrow focus on labour market participation is, as expected, insufficient to achieve the promise of egalitarian citizenship; it even falls short of tackling the social and economic structures shaping the gendered and ethnic inequalities of the labour market itself. Contextualising economic activity in the political structures of citizenship and its gendered, racial and class-based hierarchies, allows accounting for present and historical conditions. Only then can we begin articulating a vision of economic life that rejects any perceived inherent deficiency in the people made into constituencies for empowerment and inclusion by regimes predicated upon stripping them of any substantial economic and political power.

References

Abdo, N. (1992). Racism, Zionism and the Palestinian Working Class, 1920–1947. *Studies in Political Economy, 37*(1), 59–92.

Dahan-Kalev, H. (2001, November). Tensions in Israeli Feminism: The Mizrahi Ashkenazi Rift. In *Women's Studies International Forum* (Vol. 24, No. 6, pp. 669–684). Pergamon.

Hashash, Y. (2017). We're All Jews: On 'White Trash,' Mizrahim, and Intersectionality within the Hegemony. *Theory & Criticism, 48*, 249–264. (Hebrew).

Korteweg, A. C., & Yurdakul, G. (2014). *The Headscarf Debates.* Stanford University Press.

Lavie, S. (2018). *Wrapped in the Flag of Israel: Mizrahi Single Mothers and Bureaucratic Torture.* University of Nebraska Press.

Levy, D., & Weiss, Y. (2002). *Challenging Ethnic Citizenship. German and Israeli Perspectives on Immigration*. Berghahn Books.

Offer, S. (2004). The Socio-Economic Integration of the Ethiopian Community in Israel. *International Migration, 42*(3), 29–55.

Remennick, L. I. (1999). 'Women with a Russian Accent' in Israel. *European Journal of Women's Studies, 6*(4), 441–461.

Rottmann, S. B., & Ferree, M. M. (2008). Citizenship and Intersectionality: German Feminist Debates About Headscarf and Antidiscrimination Laws. *Social Politics, 15*(4), 481–513.

Shalhoub-Kevorkian, N. (2012). The Grammar of Rights in Colonial Contexts: The Case of Palestinian Women in Israel. *Middle East Law and Governance, 4*(1), 106–151.

Shalhoub-Kevorkian, N., Griecci Woodsum, A., Zu'bi, H., & Busbridge, R. (2014). Funding Pain: Bedouin Women and Political Economy in the Naqab/Negev. *Feminist Economics, 20*(4), 164–186.

Shihadeh, M., & Moadi, F. (2011). *The Education Budget and Participation of Arab Women in the Labor Market in Israel: An Analysis of Gender and Ethnicity*. Policy Paper. The Galilee Society – The Arab National Society for Health Research & Services.

Sommer, I. (2021). Recognition of Foreign Qualifications in Germany: Selectivity and Power in Re-making Professionals. *International Migration*.

Spivak, G. C. (1994). Can the Subaltern Speak? In P. Willians & L. Chrisman (Eds.), *Colonial Discourse and Post-Colonial Theory: A Reader* (pp. 66–111). Routledge.

Tatour, L. (2019). *Citizenship as Domination: Settler Colonialism and the Making of Palestinian Citizenship in Israel*. Available at SSRN 3533490.

Weiss, Y. (2002). The Golem and Its Creator, or How the Jewish Nation-State Became Multiethnic. *Challenging Ethnic Citizenship: German and Israeli Perspectives on Immigration*, 82–104.

Zoabi, H. (2009, November 28). Why Do Fewer Arab Women Have Jobs in Israel Than in Saudi Arabia? *Ha'aretz*. https://www.haaretz.com/1.5009963

CHAPTER 7

Conclusion: A Feminist Always Pays Her Debts

In March 2017, the United Nations' Commission on the Status of Women held its annual session under the theme of "women's economic empowerment". Making evident, as I was nearing the conclusion of this research, that the theme of women's economic empowerment continues enjoying global success. How are we to understand this global interest in women's economic empowerment, while social and economic inequalities continue to grow locally and globally? Which forces shape the encounter between women's empowerment and the economy and determine its meaning?

I embarked on this research with curiosity as for what the field of women's economic empowerment can disclose to us about gender and economy today; about the story of feminism in neoliberal age, and feminist encounters with vast economic inequalities persisting on intersections of gender, nationality, race, ethnicity and class, among other factors. I examined gender and economy on three levels: the macro level of citizenship as a dynamic of institutional relations among civil society, state and market; the micro level of the citizen constructed in this field; the intersection of gendered and ethno-national structures of economic citizenship. In this, I approached women's economic empowerment organisations themselves as a form of collective action, a case of civil society action aimed at repairing social and economic injustice.

One prominent story, crafted by Nancy Fraser, tells of feminism that has lost its way and collided with neoliberalism. Feminist critiques of family wage and their politicisation of the private sphere were co-opted to

I. Michaeli, *Women's Economic Empowerment*,
https://doi.org/10.1007/978-3-030-89281-4_7

serve neoliberalism and increase its appeal for women. Feminists themselves were seduced (not as passive victims, Fraser notes, but through this sophisticated co-optation) to embrace free-market individualistic empowerment and "leaning-in" instead of socialist redistribution of resources; microcredit loans instead of advocating for macro-economic policies; preoccupation with identity politics instead of persisting with social and economic justice causes.

The field of women's economic empowerment, I argued, tells a different story. Fraser is certainly right in acknowledging the entanglement of feminism and neoliberalism—indeed, a similar observation has triggered my interest in this research and it is shared by many of her critics as well. However, this rather simplistic analysis fails to do justice to feminist struggles and to account for the full complexity of their contexts of operation.

First, it is not a naïve story. In the global South, women's economic empowerment emerged as part of a radical, transformative project for social and economic justice, which assumed shifts in power relations, local and global. In countries like Israel and Germany, it emerged against the backdrop of neoliberal macro-economic policy changes that pushed low-income, indigenous, minority and immigrant women further to the margins. These are not examples of naiveté, but of painful disillusionment with the very possibility for civil society to counter the surge of neoliberal policy by the liberal means of policy lobby and advocacy. While Fraser suggested that feminists chose to neglect participatory democracy, activists testified that it was in fact the complete and utter exhaustion of that path that led them to turn to economic empowerment through micro-entrepreneurship, as it became clear that the survival of marginalised women is now their own problem, and they are on their own. More fundamentally, positioning neoliberalism and democracy (accompanied by adjectives like liberal, social or participatory) as two substantially different, if not outright oppositional venues of political action, misses out not only their present convergence, but also the historical role of democracy for capitalism (Aslan & Gambetti, 2011) and, indeed, for colonialism and the current neo-colonial economic and political world order.

Second, it is a story embedded in the changing structures of citizenship: feminist and women's rights organisations cannot be well understood when taken separately from civil society as such, and its neoliberal re-engagements with the state and the market. Questions of NGOisation of social movements, commercialisation of social economy, and co-optation of progressive agendas by both the neoliberal state and the market (including development agencies and international financial institutions) outline some of the structural conditions within which feminist and women's rights actors operate.

Certainly, civil society—including women's economic empowerment organisations—plays a central role in the production and re-production of neoliberal hegemony. I have explored this role in detail, examining the concrete mechanisms by which civil society adopts, embodies and reproduces neoliberalism: re-organisation of relationships, dependencies and power among civil society, state and market; incorporation of neoliberal means of value and judgement in the form of monitoring and evaluation frameworks; and, perhaps most blatant, the undisputed acceptance of neoclassical economics. Neoliberal hegemony is re-established in an ongoing process, through coercion as well as consent, and specifically through a set of repeated compromises of the civil society in its engagements with the state and the market. While in theory, it opens the possibility to contest neoliberalism, in practice this is complicated by the contractual form that privileges consent and compromise over conflict and confrontation, and by scientific and objective claims of neoliberal dominant regimes of truth, such as neoclassical economics indeed.

The point here is not to obscure the agency or responsibility of feminist and women's rights organisations in their different complicities with neoliberalism. Nor is it to undermine the challenges these complicities generate for gender and economic justice, and intersectional feminism (hooks, 2013; Calkin, 2015). Rather, I seek to capture and describe a political context that is in itself ambivalent and rich with internal contradictions, far from being a straightforward path with clearly defined options to choose from. As Aslan and Gambetti noted, "neoliberalism is such an ambivalent economic system that it constantly produces dilemmas to which no purely principled solution may be found" (2011: 135). And so, it is not that feminists, as Fraser has suggested, resolved their ambivalence in favour of neoliberalism, at the expense of participatory democracy and social solidarity. Closely examining the institutional relationships in this field makes visible that "resolving ambivalence" is not the appropriate rationale at all. Indeed, Chap. 3 showed while the field is rife with complex and contradictory ideologies and practices, it is set on reducing and erasing these complexities and contradictions through a great deal of means that ultimately de-politicise distinctively capitalist ways of thinking, terminologies, norms and practices, re-establishing them as value-neutral. In this field, ambivalence is not simply resolved one way or the other; it is regulated, re-signified and emptied of its internal conflict altogether.

Third, this is a story of neoliberal reconfiguration of relationship between the personal and the political, beyond mere neoliberal individualism at the expense of collective action. As Chap. 5 outlines, the actual practice of empowerment and entrepreneurship training involves a range of tools designed to transform behaviour, perception and consciousness of the participant. Understood here as a technology of citizenship, it produces citizens who act upon their wills and interests—but it also aspires to construct these very wills and interests. From this perspective, we can acknowledge that the focus on the individual is not apolitical, nor is it in itself neoliberal. Consciousness-raising and personal transformation have been key to Western second-wave radical feminism. And of course, women's rights organisations are in themselves a form of collective, rather than individualistic, action. The radical difference between consciousness-raising then and now, I argued, lies not in the focus on the personal, but in the way the relationship between the personal and the political is reconfigured. It is evident in that civil society organisations do not intend or desire that consciousness-raising on external injustices would lead to social mobilisation and collective political action; rather, it is intended to be contained within the subject. This is one of the many paradoxes in the field: women's economic empowerment organisations mostly recognise that inequalities are structural, yet the only solutions they can offer are individual.

Fourth, it is a story that ties identity and economy together. The analytical opposition socialist feminists like Fraser create between culture and economy, so that identity is primarily (even though not exclusively) relegated to the cultural sphere, does not hold in the field of women's economic empowerment. The interest of powerful institutions in economic empowerment and microcredit has been dutifully problematised, in existing literature and my own research. Yet, the interest of grassroots NGOs like ISI e.V. and AEEW in economic empowerment does emerge from recognising the key role that identity—and specifically gender, nationality, race, ethnicity, class, age, ability, etc.—plays in economic marginalisation. These organisations may not always offer explicit accounts of outright racism or discrimination in the labour market; yet, their discourse and even more so their practice clearly acknowledge that women of ethnic minorities are experiencing particular difficulties in the labour market, and have particular needs and difficulties when acting to improve their economic situation.

Consideration of historical developments and current conditions of the labour market—including entrepreneurship and access to capital and markets—illustrates how deeply economic citizenship is rooted in the gendered structures of nationality, ethnicity and class. Disempowerment runs through the social stratification of education systems, labour market structures, and other institutions embedded in ethnic citizenship regimes, with profoundly marginalising effects for ethnic minorities, indigenous peoples, migrants. I thus suggested that economic injustices are insufficiently tackled not due to exaggerated focus on identity. Quite the opposite, the problem seems to be in the insufficient focus on citizenship regimes and the core reasons for the disempowerment they perpetuate through the axes of identity—from labour market discrimination to colonial dispossession. Furthermore, the construction of the entrepreneurial self indicates clearly how neoliberal economic and political rationalities operate through normative gender roles, so that the de-stabilisation of the patriarchal heteronormative family (as evident in significant divorce rates for participants of some of the programmes, for example) produces a sense of discomfort and ambivalence in the field of women's economic empowerment.

Historicisation is also the key to going beyond empowerment and citizenship as normative concepts and desirable political projects. Critical investigations of disempowerment, be it in the labour market or the nation-state context, expose the ways in which market economies and citizenship regimes can be predicated upon exploitation and dispossession of certain populations, which then ironically find themselves targets of state-sponsored "empowerment" and "inclusion" initiatives. Simply put, a historical perspective on injustices shifts the interrogation from the well-meaning and positive-sounding terms like empowerment and inclusion, to questioning the economic and political projects and systems in which inclusion is promised.

Finally, and perhaps most importantly, it is not a neat and coherent story. Contradictions are endemic to the project of women's economic empowerment, its discourses and practices. One critic of Fraser's work rightly noted that her account "possesses a slight nostalgic quality for a coherent socialist feminist project" (Schwarz, 2013). The case of women's economic empowerment leads us to question the very possibility of such a project in this moment in history. For this reason, I am offering not a neatly crafted counter-narrative, but rather attentiveness to the multiple incoherencies and contradictions inhabiting this field, and by extension civil society. Ultimately, Fraser both underestimates and overestimates the agency of feminists and women's rights movements. The underestimation is in the failure to recognise the actual struggles that led women's rights activists to turn to microcredit and micro-entrepreneurship, which they recognised or discovered as the only remaining path accessible to them, given the failure of attempts to push back against neoliberal policies. What she overestimates is their agency, by implicitly assuming that they could have successfully resisted these neoliberal policies—if only they had tried harder! Careful attention to lived realities and challenges of grassroots organisations makes reduction, as tempting as it may be, much more difficult. It invites accountability for the immense scope and depth of challenges and obstacles facing feminists and civil society efforts of social and economic change in neoliberal times. This, I believe, is where practice-based knowledge production can inform and enrich academic research; and, where academic research can contribute to feminist struggles for social and economic justice, in a practice of solidarity.

Where do we continue from here? How do we move beyond the trap of co-optation in systems effectively built to shift institutional, interpersonal and even self-governance dynamics from coercion to consent? Throughout this book I have analysed and acknowledged how difficult it is to resist the neoliberal rules of the game, as institutional power structures, subject-making processes, citizenship ideologies, all collude in imposing dynamics of consensus. Understanding resistance as anything but lightly, the proposition I make here is to resist the will to consent. To resist the tyranny of the neoliberal consensus, or perhaps the neoliberal tyranny of consensus. It is curious that the feminist discourses on the critical importance and the urgently needed practices of consent in interpersonal relationships coincide with the rise of consensus-based technologies of power.

In contractual capitalism and in the neoliberal spirit of multi-stakeholderism, for consensus to prevail, it must be manufactured at all costs. Resistance is delegitimised. Complicity is celebrated as a form of pragmatism. Margaret Somers has argued that the Arendtian right to have rights is under attack. It well may be that in this day and age, the right to say no is under attack just as much. Yet, we continue witnessing powerful examples of resistance and refusal to be complicit, such as the anti-debt movements. South-led movements have problematised debt and structural adjustments not just for the sheer impossibility to repay them, but primarily for their illegitimacy (Baillot, 2021). They have been saying no, not only to repaying the debt, but to the entire financial architecture and ideological justification of global debt, condemning it as a form of neo-colonial exploitation and continued domination of the global North.

Catherine Eschle and Bice Maiguashca (2018) suggest that feminist critique of neoliberalism can be problematic in dividing women into age-old binaries of bad women and good women, those complicit with neoliberalism and those critical of it. I wish to somewhat reverse their analogy. Surely, we must not divide feminists into good and bad. Yet, why not embrace the bad women's imagery in paving our future paths beyond binaries of co-optation and resistance, in refusing the disciplinary temptation of becoming the "good women" that microfinance and other market and state institutions celebrate so much. This suggestion is as playful as it is serious. After all, countless feminist journeys have started with an attraction to and fascination with bad girls, despite all the grave consequences society may hold for you, when you transgress gender boundaries and social norms. When we say no, we fail to meet the expectation from women to be nice and to play, at all costs, by the neoliberal rules of consensus. We can try rejecting the positions offered to us (albeit the risks and consequences are never equal): the woman moving mountains to repay the microcredit loan at predatory percentage, the feminist sitting with a corporation at a multi-stakeholder table, the NGO practitioner diligently reporting against the M&E benchmarks that make little sense for people's lives . We can question the restrictive gender norms and the ideologies that place an absolute moral value on repayment and subjugation to predatory debt systems. Bad girls can reject the capitalist devaluation of the unemployed and the criminalised, and create counter-cultures and autonomous systems of value. Bad girls can claim both the personal and the political, can form coalitions and build collective power. As complicity and consensus mark this particular neoliberal moment, there is an abundance of powerful traditions and trajectories of feminist resistance and rebellion against economic and political oppression to inspire us. As we search for a pathway beyond binaries of complicity and resistance, resistance—firmly grounded in material realities—must still be within reach.

References

Aslan, Ö., & Gambetti, Z. (2011). Provincializing Fraser's History: Feminism and Neoliberalism Revisited. *History of the Present, 1*(1), 130–147.

Baillot, H. (2021). A Well-Adjusted Debt: How the International Anti-Debt Movement Failed to Delink Debt Relief and Structural Adjustment. *International Review of Social History, 66*(S29), 215–238.

Calkin, S. (2015). Feminism, Interrupted? Gender and Development in the Era of 'Smart Economics'. *Progress in Development Studies, 15*(4), 295–307.
Eschle, C., & Maiguashca, B. (2018). Theorising Feminist Organising in and Against Neoliberalism: Beyond Co-Optation and Resistance? *European Journal of Politics and Gender, 1*(1–2), 223–239.
hooks, b. (2013, October 28). Dig Deep: Beyond Lean In. *The Feminist Wire.* http://thefeministwire.com/2013/10/17973
Schwarz, M. (2013). Kicking Back, Not Leaning In, a Review of Fortunes of Feminism: From State-Managed Capitalism to Neoliberal Crisis by Nancy Fraser. *Dissent Magazine.* https://www.dissentmagazine.org/article/kicking-back-not-leaning-in

Index

I. Michaeli, *Women's Economic Empowerment*,
https://doi.org/10.1007/978-3-030-89281-4

The manufacturer's authorised representative in the EU is Springer Nature Customer Service Centre GmbH, Europaplatz 3, 69115 Heidelberg, Germany. If you have any concerns regarding our products, please contact ProductSafety@springernature.com

Printed and bound by CPI Group (UK) Ltd, Croydon, CR0 4YY
30/09/2026
02225475-0018